T0127023

Praise for
LIFECIRCLE LEADERSHIP

Dr. Townsend's work is a wonderfully unique blend of her philosophy, education and experience as an attorney, CEO, mentor, parent and visionary. The mission of her work is an invitation to all people to contrast sameness and differences in today's "impulse society" and to treat everyone with respect and care. She calls on everyone in the business world to utilize compassion and empathy in all relationships, regardless of corporate rank. When applied to all aspects of business (talent acquisition/development, reorganization, management, etc.), her work integrates the philosophy of working for the collective good in direct contrast to "every man (woman) for himself." In my opinion, Dr. Townsend's Lifecircle Leadership *is a work for everyone. We can apply her call to action daily in pursuit of meaning and purpose outside of ourselves.*

DR. NICK MOLINARO
Principal, Champion's Mind

Dr. Kim Townsend has synthesized insights from her diverse professional experiences into an important book on leadership. A must-read for leaders.

JOHN CAPASSO
Executive Vice President, Continuing Care Group, Trinity Health

Kimberly Townsend has written a must-read book for anyone who wants to live their best life and have a positive mental attitude daily. Read this book—and learn from one of the best.

PHYLLIS W. NEWHOUSE
Chief Executive Officer, Xtreme Solutions, Inc.

Lifecircle
LEADERSHIP

Lifecircle
LEADERSHIP

HOW EXCEPTIONAL
PEOPLE MAKE EVERY DAY
EXTRAORDINARY

DR. KIMBERLY TOWNSEND

Copyright © 2018 by Kimberly Townsend.

All rights reserved. No part of this book may be used or reproduced in any manner whatsoever without prior written consent of the author, except as provided by the United States of America copyright law.

Published by Advantage, Charleston, South Carolina.
Member of Advantage Media Group.

ADVANTAGE is a registered trademark, and the Advantage colophon is a trademark of Advantage Media Group, Inc.

Printed in the United States of America.

10 9 8 7 6 5 4 3 2 1

ISBN: 978-1-59932-9215
LCCN: 2018958241

Book design by Carly Blake.

This publication is designed to provide accurate and authoritative information in regard to the subject matter covered. It is sold with the understanding that the publisher is not engaged in rendering legal, accounting, or other professional services. If legal advice or other expert assistance is required, the services of a competent professional person should be sought.

Advantage Media Group is proud to be a part of the Tree Neutral® program. Tree Neutral offsets the number of trees consumed in the production and printing of this book by taking proactive steps such as planting trees in direct proportion to the number of trees used to print books. To learn more about Tree Neutral, please visit **www.treeneutral.com**.

Advantage Media Group is a publisher of business, self-improvement, and professional development books and online learning. We help entrepreneurs, business leaders, and professionals share their Stories, Passion, and Knowledge to help others Learn & Grow. Do you have a manuscript or book idea that you would like us to consider for publishing? Please visit **advantagefamily.com** or call **1.866.775.1696**.

To my husband, John, and our children and grandchildren. Without their support, encouragement, patience and sense of humor, I would not be able to fulfill my life purpose in leadership. To my late father, Nelson Menard, who shared a lot of pithy life wisdom with me. Some of his advice is publishable, but not his most useful and memorable insights.

TABLE OF CONTENTS

FOREWORD

n all aspects of my life—daughter, sister, wife, mother, employer, and community leader—I have long held the maxim:

Don't tell me what you believe, show me what you do, and I'll know what you believe.

In other words, actions speak louder than words. Actions that include implementing programs and policies, but also active listening, displaying compassion and empathy, taking the time to pay attention and to show up and be there. People may hear what you say but it's your actions that will define your true character.

For the past twenty years, I've served as executive director of the Allyn Foundation, a charitable organization committed to improving the quality of life in Central New York. The foundation was started in 1954 with its roots in the company Welch Allyn. It was in the halls of Welch Allyn that I first met Kim Townsend.

The culture of Welch Allyn was embodied in its core value, Be Always Kind and True. As a family owned business, the owners were employee-centric, and every employee felt that they were not just a worker but a member of a larger family. My husband, a member of the Allyn family, would walk through the manufacturing floor and not only know peoples' names, but also their family history and stories.

As part of the legal department at Welch Allyn, Kim was part of this family and culture. She embodied the spirit of the company and continued her life-long learning by earning an MPA and an MBA while working full-time as a corporate lawyer.

Now at the helm of a multi-million-dollar organization, Kim faces the challenges and financial pressures of running a complex and multi-faceted company. Her solution to thriving both as a CEO and a company is to be kind to yourself and others. Based upon Kim's extensive academic, personal and professional experiences, she eloquently explains how personal satisfaction and personal fulfillment can be found in simply doing good...for yourself, for your fellow employees and for your community.

Kim's vision for her company and our community is embodied in a concept of "pragmatic altruism" in which we see every employee and every client as a human being with potential and opportunity. All too often, employers view employees as almost robots; just get the job done. As Kim highlights, a better business strategy and a better human strategy is to recognize the interconnectedness of employees' work lives and personal lives. With sound advice and concrete examples, Kim compels leaders and employers to embrace and practice a spirit of pragmatic altruism because it's good for the bottom line of business and good for employees.

Everyone has a story and Dr. Kim Townsend's personal and professional journey are the root of her philosophy. The challenges and obstacles she faced are real and are at the heart of her core values. Now, as a leader, she is the voice calling for change. Her passionate plea for empathetic leadership presents a new paradigm that combines common good and good business. It's a call to action: if we want to live in a world in which people are kind to each other then let's all start following Kim's example. Embrace Lifecircle Leadership.

Meg O'Connell

Executive Director

Allyn Foundation

INTRODUCTION

The initial concept for this book found its genesis in a doctoral thesis I wrote in 2015 as part of the requirements for the doctor of education degree I earned through the executive leadership program at the Ralph C. Wilson School of Education at St. John Fisher College.

The thesis was entitled "Leading for Good in the Impulse Society" and examined the complex role of an executive at a time in our collective history when technological advancements, shifts in social strata, and changes in corporate agendas have all combined to heighten the expectations placed upon a position that was already mentally, physically, and spiritually taxing enough.

The Impulse Society was the titular concept developed by journalist Paul Roberts in his brilliant 2014 book that examined the current effect and likely long-term implications of a Western society whose actions were no longer the product of reasoned and rational thought, but instead were reflexive spasms responding to momentary impulses. In this seminal work, Roberts painted a disturbingly accurate portrait of a general public that demands instant gratification of each and every passing desire, while at the same time realizing diminishing returns from the (largely) wasted efforts expended to satisfy this insatiable social appetite.

Roberts projected that over time, the collective impact of this significant social trend that found each and every individual seeking their own satisfaction without any consideration for a shared "common good" would be a significant erosion of many of the institutions and principles that had previously served as a vital societal foundation.

At the time that I came across Roberts's insightful book, I was not only deep in the midst of my doctoral work, but I had just accepted an appointment as president and chief executive officer at Loretto, a comprehensive, continuing healthcare organization that provides a variety of services throughout Central New York.

Given these momentous events in my own life, my interpretations of Roberts's persuasive arguments understandably found easy application to my personal experiences in a relatively new position of leadership that carried with it a seemingly endless array of professional demands, every one of which brought with it unexpressed expectations not only of an immediate response, but also a final resolution that satisfied all interested parties.

The first outlines I drew up for this project reflected a focus on Roberts's concept of *The Impulse Society* and these often-overwhelming pressures that are placed on an executive's shoulders. The intention here was to write a book that would serve not only as a survival guide for management drowning in the modern morass of twenty-first-century business, but would also offer an alternative narrative map that would blaze a better personal path toward an ultimate destination of a "common good," rather than individual satisfaction.

I was sincerely passionate about the proposition.

Still, as I worked through outline after outline, draft after draft, my focus gradually evolved as my once-new responsibilities at Loretto quickly became my day-to-day. Over this time, I developed personal relationships, not only with the other management professionals in the executive suite, but also with many employees at all position-designations within the company—and with many of the residents and program participants whom we are privileged to serve, as well.

After some time, what began to resonate most strongly with me weren't necessarily Roberts's somewhat esoteric observations or even my primarily academic applications of the same, but rather I was struck by the undeniable interconnectedness of all the different people with whom I came into contact with over the course of any given day. I don't mean simply the bureaucratic bonds and tethers existing between all coworkers, rather I had discovered the dependency we all had on one another in a very real-world way that extended far beyond the set boundaries of the workplace.

From this spark, I not only began to reexamine my professional position and personal responsibilities at Loretto, but also to consider my company's place within our hometown of Syracuse and the surrounding communities of Upstate New York, where our corporation serves both as one of the largest employers in the region and as a care provider to a significant number of our area's most challenged citizens. This active reconsideration on my part led me to new conclusions about what I wanted to accomplish as the president and CEO of a major corporation and, perhaps even more importantly, simply as a human being seeking to maximize the effectiveness of my life in making a real and sustainable impact on the world around me.

Although Loretto's quality of care and "bottom line" performance was and will always remain the top priorities for me, this introspection led me time and again back to the personal relationships that not only provided a certain framework for my life, but also provided me with the sort of satisfaction and fulfillment that I believe is an absolutely necessary component for anyone wishing to derive meaning from this life.

The experiences I gained from those individual relationships significantly expanded my original perspective and, with it, my approach to this particular project. Inspired by this renewed and broader outlook on the subject matter before me, I rethought my intentions and came to the realization that this project had evolved far beyond addressing those issues that were strictly limited to those of us in upper management and who may feel overwhelmed by those debilitating demands that Roberts had identified as the contagious symptoms of *The Impulse Society*—and which I frequently suffered from in my own day-to-day.

To the contrary, rather than being limited to these upper echelons, I repeatedly found that the intensifying negative impact of those factors described in Roberts's *Impulse Society* had leached out beyond the corporate boardrooms and C-class executive suites. Those same personally incapacitating effects of ever-increasing career demands had spread like a virus throughout the workforce. As a result, this shared sense of stress was (unfortunately) one of the many elements of common-footing upon which I was able to bond with my employees at absolutely all levels.

Everyone I talked to felt as if they were running too long and too hard on a proverbial "hamster wheel" at work. Not only were they all getting more and more exhausted with every turn of the wheel, but they also felt as if they were realizing continually diminishing rewards in return for the ever-increasing effort.

And so, I went back to my previous outlines and drafts, put them all aside … and I started over.

Or, rather, I went about the business of expanding my original work in order to ensure that my final product was much more inclusive in addressing a readership that I now recognized included *all* my employees, not just my fellow executives.

What you hold in your hands now is the result of all of those revisions, a book that is still intent on addressing the pressing concerns of executives and upper management as the corporate climate seems to be growing evermore demanding with each quarter. At the same time, however, these pages were written with the specific intention of being far more inclusive than was originally conceived.

The underlying concept of my final product is simple enough: Rather than be mindless participants in the ever-intensifying negativity that Roberts described was the ultimate and inevitable destination of *The Impulse Society*, each of us has within our grasp the opportunity to find professional satisfaction and personal fulfillment in simply doing good.

> Each of us has within our grasp the opportunity to find professional satisfaction and personal fulfillment in simply doing good.

For yourself.
For your fellow employees.
For your community.
Even for the world as a whole.
And all it takes is just doing good.

Doing good extends to not just your business but also your soul. It's about embodying selflessness and combining that with strategy—pragmatic altruism. I am well aware that this simple statement in "doing good" is a bold proclamation to make—especially in the days of *The Impulse Society* when "*I want what I want and I want it now!*" seems to remain the oft-repeated mantra for a voracious, but insatiate majority.

I am sure there will be many who will read my words and snort cynically at such hypothesis. They will, I imagine, dismiss my arguments out-of-hand as being naïve or trite or Pollyannaish. (Probably all three.)

Perhaps this is to be expected. The old-world notions about the competitive nature of profit and success that lead such people to mistake jadedness for acumen are deeply ingrained in our corporate culture, but they are fatally flawed. This particular brand of negative thinking is not only fertile soil for the sort of social deterioration about which Roberts warns us, but also creates significant liabilities for the "bottom line" in the long run—whether that's on a corporate or personal level. A wicked irony.

And so, I invite you to turn the page and begin your own independent process of reconsidering the various elements of your own career and personal life and—maybe, just maybe—you too will arrive at the same conclusions that I have: doing good is good business as long as you embody pragmatic altruism—to stay grounded through selflessness and practical solutions.

1

The More Things Change

Before we begin our exploration of the personal and professional potential to be found in what I have come to refer to as pragmatic altruism, I believe there is an underlying need to take a moment for reflection on the current state of affairs in which we find ourselves, plummeting into the depths of what Roberts described in *The Impulse Society*.

Tragedy and misfortune, cruelty and hostility—they are not anything new to this world. The annals of history often seem a collection of events that amount to little more than a game of one-upmanship in man's inhumanity to man. I would even be reticent to suggest that our society has ever truly enjoyed a period of what could legitimately be termed civility, especially where that same historical record is filled with examples of terrible prejudice and pettiness.

While I largely agree with Roberts's conclusions regarding a negative social trajectory, I am aware that there is no real "Golden Age" when times were as good as some may mistakenly remember, but neither am I one of those bitter folks who ball their fists in furious frustration and shake it at the heavens above, cursing, "kids today!"

Life has always had a significant negativity to it. It's just the way that it is. At the same time, while the horrors and injustices that seem to be inextricably interwoven with the wonders of this world continue on as they always have ... I believe that something's different in the world today.

Not necessarily dramatically altered. Sometimes, almost imperceptibly divergent from our shared norm. But ... *different*. Often in a way that defies articulation, but different, nevertheless.

I'm not alone in my observation. From board meetings to charity events, and from time spent with my family to conversations with my coworkers, it seems that everyone these days is quick to observe that things are *different* now.

And not in a good way. Certainly not getting any better.

Technology is, of course, most often fingered as the "usual suspect" to blame for it all, but I think that's unfair—or, at least, an incomplete explanation.

When I began my legal career as a student at Syracuse University, College of Law (not long ago), our law library boasted a massive book collection that was contained in a separate building, several floors high and with a cavernous basement. Even then, the library was more regionally focused and far from offering what anyone might think of as a complete collection of legal references. And performing the required legal research in this massive archive was a time-consuming and laborious endeavor.

All that has changed.

Today, just a short time later, the smart phone I can hold comfortably in my hand can not only access the complete legal database of the entire United States over the whole of its history, but it can do the same for every other nation on earth. And the research is done for me in a matter of seconds.

Yet the incredible access to information that technology has provided has been a double-edged sword.

The cell phone that contains almost immediate access to the world's legal resources also allows me the freedom to leave my office and

> Yet the incredible access to information that technology has provided has been a double-edged sword.

yet stay connected in a meaningful way. At the same time, however, this "instrument of freedom" is also the same device that keeps me tethered to the office 24/7—even after I've left the building. Technology that gives me a certain degree of freedom also makes me "available" to intrusions into what would have been regarded as my personal time in a pre-cell phone era.

In the same way, video conferencing allows for necessary meetings to take place with a simulated face-to-face, without the need for all the hassles and expenses of business travel. Plus, my personal favorite, emails make it possible to transmit not just a single document or two but limitless volumes across miles without any time delay or expense, whereas standard mail was slow, expensive, and often unreliable.

The costly flip-side to all these technological advances, however, is that there is absolutely no more separation or geographical distance. Every single office in the world is, for all intents and purposes, the "office right next door," and there no longer exists any good reason why this file or that project can't be put up on someone else's screen immediately. And therein lies the problem.

Immediately.

The timetable on everything has shrunken from merely "rushed" to "immediately, if not sooner." And that change has had a dramatic impact on the American workplace.

Where the international standard for hours worked is a national point of pride and our fast pace and high stress have long been every bit as iconic of the United States as baseball and apple pie, the emotional environment within the average workplace has become even more intense. And, perhaps even worse, that pressure is no longer something that the average worker can leave behind in the office and shake off over the course of their commute home. No, technology has provided us with a means of taking all of those demands home with us.

Weekend teleconferences. Midnight emails. E-hovering while on vacation. None of these are unusual occurrences in twenty-first-century corporate America.

And the real-world consequences of these intensifying pressures are by no means relegated to the stuff of esoteric and academic considerations. No, their real-world effect is all too painfully clear in the everyday lives of far too many. Here are a few examples:

> More than half of all Americans reported that they were unhappy at work.

- A recent *Forbes*[1] article stated that more than half of all Americans reported they were unhappy at work.

- According to the American Psychological Association, between 40–50 percent of marriages end in divorce.[2]

---

1   Susan Adams, "Most Americans Are Unhappy At Work," *Forbes*, Forbes Magazine, June 20, 2014, www.forbes.com/sites/susanadams/2014/06/20/most-americans-are-unhappy-at-work/#469834ad341a.

2   American Psychological Association, "Marriage and Divorce," *Monitor on Psychology*, www.apa.org/topics/divorce.

- The dramatic rise in incidents of alcoholism among American women—including, a doubling of alcohol-related deaths since 1999—has been largely attributed to the rise of women to levels of authority within the workplace.[3]

- According to the Anxiety and Depression Association of America, anxiety is the most commonly diagnosed mental illness, with over 40 million Americans identified as suffering from the condition. And Major Depression Disorder is the number one cause of disability among Americans with more than 16 million sufferers.[4]

- And while technology has gifted us with medical care that has never been more advanced or sophisticated, the fact remains that the life expectancy in America has dropped and continues to drop.[5] This is largely as a result of an opioid epidemic that is not restricted to conventional conclusions and stereotypes about drug addicts but extends into the most affluent of areas and the most distinguished of professional arenas. In fact, as OxyContin and other prescriptive opioids become increasingly more expensive and more strictly regulated, the migration to heroin—once considered the ultimate "street drug"—is now led by white, college-educated suburbanites.[6]

---

3   Bridget F. Grant, "Prevalence of Alcohol Use, High-Risk Drinking, and DSM-IV Alcohol Use Disorder," *JAMA Internal Medicine*, Sept. 1, 2017, jamanetwork.com/journals/jamapsychiatry/article-abstract/2647079.

4   Anxiety and Depression Association of America, "Facts & Statistics," *ADAA*, adaa.org/about-adaa/press-room/facts-statistics.

5   Aimee Cunningham, "U.S. Life Expectancy Drops for the Second Year in a Row," *Science News*, Dec. 21, 2017, www.sciencenews.org/blog/science-ticker/us-life-expectancy-drops-second-year.

6   Amy Norton, "Today's Heroin Abusers Often Middle Class: Study," *WebMD*, WebMD, May 28, 2014, www.webmd.com/mental-health/addiction/news/20140528/todays-heroin-abusers-often-middle-class-suburbanites-study#1.

"And what of it?" my jaded friends would ask. In this dog eat dog world, life is hard. *Right?* And business is even harder. *Right?* It's every man (or woman) for himself and if you can't stand the heat, get out of the kitchen.

And of all the effects of social deterioration that we are currently witnessing, this particular outlook of cold indifference may be the most dramatic and most tragic impact of them all. It's no mere subjective observation. Scientific studies have documented conclusively that levels of empathy have declined among college-educated Americans since the 1980s—and they continue to fall.[7]

Now, my more jaded friends would certainly dismiss my concerns about levels of empathy as being soft and of no significance to business matters, but that is precisely the problem. This lack of concern that so many now demonstrate for one another's well-being prevents them from considering and understanding the real-world costs of those conditions.

That's right … real world costs. Money.

So, while it might be easy at first to dismiss me as one of those "dreamers" (and I freely confess to knowing and believing in many of the lyrics of John Lennon's "Imagine"), the fact of the matter is that as an attorney and President/CEO of a corporation that earns significant annual revenues, I can see the dollars and cents behind—or, maybe, in addition to—the terrible human costs. It's not an either/or proposition.

Add to this the disturbing fact that the amount of prescription anti-depressants and anti-anxiety medicines are so prevalent in American society that their presence in the water supply as a result of

---

7   Maia Szalavitz, "Shocker: Empathy Dropped 40% in College Students Since 2000," *Psychology Today*, www.psychologytoday.com/us/blog/born-love/201005/ shocker-empathy-dropped-40-in-college-students-2000.

simple human excretion has negatively impacted fishing resources in the Pacific, Atlantic, and Great Lakes, or that the tap water of most municipal water supplies also contains the medicines.[8] The Harvard Medical School has identified that workers suffering from anxiety and/or depression are more likely to miss additional work and contribute less when they are present. Moreover, that same study showed that these conditions in C-level executives led them to take fewer risks, which significantly compromised their abilities to realize and take full advantage of opportunities when presented.[9]

The Gallup Company recently published a poll that suggested that worker dissatisfaction cost the American economy more than $405–$505 billion every year.[10] That's no typo … *billions*. A year. And that cost is rising steadily.

The Council of Economic Advisers, a part of the Executive Office of the President, has estimated that in 2015, the total cost of the opioid crisis to the American economy was $504 billion.[11]

Not to be outdone, the Center for Disease Control and Prevention (CDC) has estimated that the similar annual cost to the American economy related to excessive alcohol consumption is close to $250 billion.[12]

I could go on, but the inescapable conclusion is clear: While I

---

8   Bruce Y. Lee, "Antidepressants Found in the Great Lakes And Fish," *Forbes Magazine*, Sept. 5, 2017, www.forbes.com/sites/brucelee/2017/09/04/ antidepressants-found-in-the-great-lakes-and-fish/#26f4cc6587db.

9   Harvard Health Publishing. "Mental Health Problems in the Workplace" *Harvard Health Blog*, www.health.harvard.edu/newsletter_article/ mental-health-problems-in-the-workplace.

10   Catherine Clifford, "Unhappy Workers Cost the U.S. Up to $550 Billion a Year (Infographic)," *Entrepreneur*, May 10, 2015, www.entrepreneur.com/article/246036.

11   US Government, "Council of Economic Advisers Report: The Underestimated Cost of the Opioid Crisis," *The White House*, www.whitehouse.gov/briefings-statements/ cea-report-underestimated-cost-opioid-crisis/.

12   Centers for Disease Control and Prevention, "Alcohol and Public Health," *Centers for Disease Control and Prevention*, Mar. 27, 2018, www.cdc.gov/alcohol/index.htm.

don't make any effort to conceal my humanity or compassion, there is nothing Pollyannaish in my concern for the well-being of everyone within my offices, workplace, and community—*everybody*.

There is nothing "soft" in being concerned about worsening conditions that currently cost the American economy more than $5 billion.

The time has come to reconsider how we approach not only business, but one another. The time has come to embrace Lifecircle Leadership's philosophy: doing good is good business. But it's not just doing good, it's also caring for yourself, your company, your community, and getting out from under the constant pressure of our "instant-on" society, in a meaningful, but realistic way—this is the heart of pragmatic altruism. It's not doing good for good's sake, but with a vision, a purpose, and in a way that's a "win-win" for yourself and your business.

And the time to get started is now.

2

You

Anyone who has ever flown on a commercial aircraft has seen the same safety demonstration.

"In case of a lack of cabin pressure … ." We all know the drill, including the dire admonition that comes as a conclusion. "Make sure to fasten and secure your own mask before attempting to assist those around you." Good advice, I say.

It may seem inconsistent in a book focused on doing good for others for me to so brazenly advocate that everyone take care of themselves first, but there's a perfectly sound reason behind this.

The reason you want to put your mask on first isn't due simply to primitive survival instinct. Rather, the practice follows the simple fact that you can't help your fellow passengers if you yourself have passed out.

> If you're not your best self, then you can't help those who directly count on you.

The same principle applies to life. If you're not your best self, then you can't help those who directly count on you : your significant other, kids, parents, etc.

More than that, however, you can't make a full contribution to your workplace, which places an additional strain on that environment. And so on. I learned this particular lesson the same way I have picked up too many of the pieces of my personal trophy trove of wisdom: experience.

When I assumed my position as president/CEO at Loretto, it certainly wasn't the first high-pressure post that I had held. And by that, I don't reference the stature, responsibility, or compensation that might typically come to mind.

To the contrary, my career has been a long, hard climb out of the depths of being undereducated and underemployed. Many of the positions that carried the most stress for me were not the ones I held as an attorney or executive, but were the extra jobs that I took to pay the bills and take care of my children.

I worked multiple jobs. Evenings and weekends, while finishing my degree. Then going to law school. And through it all, I was taking care of my kids. Always taking care of my kids. None of that makes me the slightest bit special. I did what I did to provide for my kids and to ensure that their futures were as bright as they could possibly be. That's all.

And now that I am president/CEO, I go to work with women and men who are doing the same exact thing, day-in and day-out. Their circumstances may be different from mine, but I recognize in each and every one of them the very same nose-to-the-grindstone intent that I have always held in my heart. And I recognize their determination to provide for their children and their children's future.

That's just about as "high-pressured" as life can get.

While I don't regret any of the hard work that my ascending career path required of me, I am aware that I developed some very natural, but ultimately unhealthy practices along the way. Chief among these was always putting everyone else's needs and desires before my own: My children. My employers. My coworkers. Everyone.

For me personally, the result of my compulsion to take care of others, no matter the personal costs to me, left me frequently depleted of the very qualities and abilities I needed to fully satisfy my enormous responsibilities to take care of others. (One of life's painful little ironies.)

It wasn't long into my tenure at Loretto, however, that I recognized those very same symptoms in far too many of our own employees.

Here were good people who were simply giving too much of themselves.

Certainly, nothing about that aspect of my situation changed for me as I climbed the corporate ladder and my employment positions improved. If anything, I discovered that the higher I climbed, the greater the demands that were placed upon me and the stronger my compulsion to put others before me.

And I had less and less to give.

I know I'm not alone in feeling that way. The same scenario plays out with all too many people today. It's not that they don't care about their responsibilities to family or workplace or community. Just the opposite, in fact. I think the demands of The Impulse Society are so great that it is increasingly easy to overextend one's personal collateral and simply burn out.

That is when the metaphorical cabin pressure drops dangerously low and all of those who had worried about getting the oxygen masks on every other passengers in the plane black out; unable to help anyone, including themselves.

There have certainly been more than a few times that I have felt "dizzy" under the collection of my burdens. And looking back over the trials, tribulations, and obstacles I have overcome, I don't necessarily feel as strong or empowered at having survived them all as I do feeling just plain lucky. Or blessed.

What changed for me—and I think it was probably more a matter of necessity than the election of an option—was the discovery of a sense of balance in my life.

There is a point at which selflessness becomes selfish, and selfishness becomes selfless.

> There is a point at which selflessness becomes selfish, and selfishness becomes selfless.

I would never suggest depriving those in your life of anything they need, particularly your children. I have learned over the years, however, that there is an important and very necessary distinction to be drawn between *needs* and *desires*.

What I mean by this is that children *need* a safe environment—good food, clean water. They don't necessarily need a certain pair of sneakers or particular brand of clothes. Those are merely desires—no matter how loudly they yowl.

In the same way, your employer needs you to perform your work duties with your maximum effort and to the best of your abilities. They don't necessarily need you to comply with every unreasonable request. Those are merely desires. And while the needs of others sometimes can't be overlooked or denied, it is shortsighted to sacrifice your own needs to satisfy the desires of others.

It is essential that you recognize your own personal worth and make an investment in yourself and your future, not only for your own welfare, but for those within your circle of care and benevolence.

While I'm certain that my kids would have preferred that my attention (and income) was focused on them, I made such an investment in myself when I directed both time and financial resources in pursuit of my own education.

In the end, the opportunities created as a result of having earned my education allowed me to realize my personal goals, and also to better provide for my children—including fulfilling many of their desires to an extent I never could have done if I hadn't made those sacrifices and redirected my resources to myself.

At the same time, I never once let my educational pursuits interfere with any of my professional duties. My dedication to my studies frequently made it necessary to prioritize my energies to create definable borders for my professional responsibilities to ensure that these did not bleed over into the personal time I needed to set aside for my academic endeavors.

I don't think there is any question that the education I acquired along the way, together with the personal growth that accompanied these achievements, made me a much better employee and increased my overall performance in the workplace.

Balance.

This I learned, often through a long struggle with a situation complicated by one imbalanced element or another, was (and is) the key to my personal progression and well-being and to the direct benefit of those who depended upon me. I could only give of myself if those generous acts of bestowing upon others did not deplete my own resources.

The example that I have offered is my education, but the actual application of this principle certainly presented itself in every other aspect of my life as well, even the most fundamental—perhaps, in those elements most of all.

For example, with all of the pressures and time demands that we face in our professional and personal lives, it is all too easy to lapse into behaviors that seem necessary in the moment, but which are extremely detrimental in the long run. A healthy diet. Sufficient sleep. Regular exercise. All of these are needs, not desires. Still, these are among the first items that we sacrifice in order to accommodate the needs of others. I know I am guilty.

I'd be the last person to say that I don't understand that special circumstances occasionally necessitate those types of sacrifices, but they become more problematic when those events transition from emergency accommodations to patterns of behavior. In those instances, the body eventually gives way to the extraordinary strain and begins to slow down, then to break down. Judgment begins to become impaired and performance suffers.

In the end, the sacrifices undertaken to accommodate extraordinary situations leave us less capable of handling even our normal demands, especially impacting personal relationships. Healthy, happy, and satisfying human relationships with a significant other, children, family, and/or friends are not simply among the most rewarding aspects of our life, they are a basic need of that existence.

All too often, I have seen well-intentioned individuals put extraordinary pressures upon themselves at work, all so that they can provide for their family and loved ones. The painful irony here is that, frequently, what they sacrifice to accomplish all of this is the relationships with those people whom they're work so hard to satisfy. In

> Healthy, happy, and satisfying human relationships with a significant other, children, family, and/or friends are not simply among the most rewarding aspects of our life, they are a basic need of that existence.

the end, all sides wind up with a collection of "stuff," but without the types of human contacts and relationships that are necessary to maintaining a healthy life—and to continuing to be a productive person.

We human beings are social animals by design. We need to interact with others, to be a part of our community and to contribute to its success and perpetuation.

One of the most serious complications of The Impulse Society is the increasing isolation that too many of us feel today. As we retreat into our personal devices and online existence, the human interactions inevitably suffer. And we suffer with them.

If we as human beings are going to live healthy, happy, productive lives, it's essential that we take care of ourselves—but that alone is not enough. We must also take care of others.

And so again, what might easily be dismissed as a soft and emotional concern is really the rational recognition of a stone-cold fact. The best thing we can do for ourselves is to do good for others.

3

Begin at the Beginning

E verything begins at the beginning.

At first, that may seem obvious, but I suggest you consider this more deeply.

When I arrived for my very first morning at Loretto, I settled into my nicely appointed office, with all the expected executive accoutrements and the best view that the building could offer and began my service as the head of a multi-million-dollar corporation.

Or, that is how it might have seemed to the casual observer.

The fact of the matter is that I didn't just walk into that corner office as if I had been birthed anew from the ether, appearing out of nowhere and then occupying that seat at the very head of the company.

To the contrary, there had been a long journey before I reached that particular point of achievement. I had served for an extended period of time on Loretto's board of directors, becoming intimately familiar with the company's polices, practices, procedures, and underlying culture. This had included, of course, introductions and interactions with the other board members, corporate executives, and other top personnel.

Finding my way onto Loretto's board of directors had come as a direct result of my work with Welch Allyn and the Allyn Family Foundation, a charitable foundation deeply involved in a number of similar entities throughout the greater Upstate New York region.

Before that, I had served in a number of positions as an attorney, positions I secured in no small part as a direct result of my academic performance at Syracuse University, College of Law. My point is that I did not take my seat as president/CEO of Loretto as a completely new individual, but rather I assumed that post as an assemblage of all the cobbled-together parts of the entirety of my life experiences, including—without wanting to delve into the depths of a Freudian and/or Jungian tangent here—the events of my childhood.

I am not unique in that regard.

All of us are products of all of those hundreds and thousands of life experiences that lead from that beginning I've mentioned right up to the places that we currently occupy and the situations in which we presently find ourselves. That's undeniable; just the impact of linear time.

For many, however—I think particularly for those who occupy upper-management and executive positions—there is an almost irresistible temptation to disregard this silent lineage and focus solely on the events of the day and on meeting the demands of the future. Certainly understandable, yet a potentially disastrous practice to undertake.

The Peabody award-winning broadcaster Bergen Baldwin Evans wrote in his *The Natural History of Nonsense* (1946), "We may be through with the past, but the past is not through with us."[13] (The quote is more commonly remembered from the narration of Paul Thomas Anderson's film, *Magnolia* (1999).) This is undeniably true.

---

13   Bergen Evans, *The Natural History of Nonsense* (New York: Random House, 1947).

C-level executives take their seat in their ergonomically engineered chair behind their designer desks, ready to take on all of the challenges of positions for which they've studied and worked, struggled and sacrificed, over the course of a lifetime. And yet they almost never understand that they share that posture-improving chair with all the other versions of themselves that played a part in their ascendancy.

Yes, it's a crowded chair.

The plain fact is that not all those past experiences were good or beneficial, and not all of the various versions of the individual are cooperative toward achieving the goals and agendas that those executives have set for themselves. Bad habits. Old traumas. Negative interactions.

All of these, even the most seemingly inconsequential occurrences, have a tendency to build up over time, often without our being aware of them or paying them any particular attention. And as individual events, they might as well be dismissed or overlooked, but taken all together, they can create significant performance issues where they operate collectively upon the subconscious. In the end, these otherwise inconsequential events and elements can have an extremely detrimental impact upon the individual so-afflicted, impairing the razor-sharp judgment and hindering the exceptional performance that made the success possible in the first place.

I know this to be true, because I am speaking here of personal experience.

When I assumed my role at Loretto, there were no questions concerning my qualifications and I was more than confident that I could not only justify the board of directors' faith in appointing me, but also that I could far exceed their lofty visions for the company's future.

While my qualifications and confidence were not in question, I was still aware that the physical and emotional wear-and-tear on me personally was more significant than I hoped it would be as I first envisioned myself holding that position and then fulfilling those responsibilities far into the future.

Nothing was wrong, per se, but I still recognized that something needed to be done to optimize my efforts.

Ironically, it was the fact that nothing was "wrong" that made finding a solution so much more difficult. Our natural outlook in these matters is largely focused on fixing things that are broken and ignoring those others that work just well enough and are merely in need of a minor tweak here or there to work even better.

I can now look back over my early career and see that this was the case for so many of the more senior professionals and executives with whom I worked. Nothing was broken, but in retrospect, I can now see that their performance (and occasionally their demeanor) indicated that they were in need of a good tweaking.

I count myself as remarkably fortunate to have found for myself a solution.

As I said, I knew nothing was "broken" and the situation did not merit a physician or more focused clinician, but I was immediately intrigued when someone first broached the possibility of retaining a performance professional. An executive coach.

I have heard the long litany of old sayings comparing business with this athletic event or that, but I don't think I ever considered business—my particular pursuit—as a sport until I had the great privilege of meeting Dr. Nick Molinaro.

Dr. Nick may be best known to viewers of The Golf Channel for the pro performance golf tips that he shares regularly with viewers, but he is equally well regarded for his work with numerous championship sports teams and elite athletes, and for his work that reaches far beyond the fairways and playing fields.

A licensed clinical psychologist, Dr. Nick has expanded his practice to embrace people from the world's greatest athletes to C-level executives to highly acclaimed artists by recognizing the common threads that run through all human performance, no matter what the pursuit.

For example, whether you are standing on the green with a simple ten-foot putt to win the game or sitting in the executive's chair formulating a business plan, both activities come down to the same fundamental components.

The first of these is the ability to focus on the task at hand. For many of us, our attention can drift at critical moments, whether that distraction comes in the form of growing anxiety on the green or an intensifying sense of insecurity in the boardroom. Human performance is determined first and foremost by the ability to concentrate and focus on the essential task at hand without being distracted by fears or other negative thoughts.

> Whether you are standing on the green with a simple ten-foot putt to win the game or sitting in the executive's chair formulating a business plan, both activities come down to the same fundamental components.

This, of course, is tied to the second necessary element: the ability to not only tolerate stressful situations, but to thrive in the pressure cooker. The most successful athletes are not necessarily those who can hit the ball the farthest, any more than the most successful executives are always the smartest or most imaginative people in the room. There are countless stories of athletic and entrepreneurial talents that went underutilized or unrealized altogether simply because those so endowed did not have the ability to handle the stress that came as a part of their risk/reward-heightened endeavors.

And finally, perhaps most important of all, is to integrate this focus and personal grit into the sort of decisiveness that is essential to success at any level, both on the playing field and in the office.

When I began my work with Dr. Nick, he put me through a series of tests that allowed him to more clearly identify my various personality traits and zero-in on those aspects of my executive performance that needed tweaking.

What he found took me by surprise, although once he began his explanation, the only shock became that I hadn't identified the problem by myself and much sooner.

Dr. Nick concluded that I had unreasonably high expectations of my performance. I had always regarded my pursuit of optimal performance as a personal strength. It was the trait that allowed me to worker harder than anyone else in school and to stay later at the office until everything within my responsibility was … well, perfect.

Dr. Nick, however, pointed out that while there was nothing inherently wrong with wanting to be the best I could be, the expectation of peak performance 100 percent of the time had driven me to a dangerous level of self-reliance. Because I was not willing to tolerate any mistakes, I was less likely to delegate responsibility, often taking more on my own shoulders than I could comfortably manage.

Through a series of exercises that Dr. Nick put me through, I was able to recognize that my innate unreasonably high self-expectations were actually interfering with my performance as Loretto's president/CEO.

Letting go of that unrealistic standard removed an enormous amount of pressure from every task I faced during the course of my day, and with that new-gained freedom, I felt empowered to face my remaining stressors like a champion.

Moreover, without my ever-present fear of imperfection, I was better able to focus on the more important aspects of the day-to-day tasks already in front of me.

Perhaps most important, because each and every decision no longer offered the daunting prospect of perfection-or-failure, I discovered that my decision-making skills improved significantly. Along with that marked advantage, I found that my newly won tolerance for an acceptable level of imperfection (or humanity) allowed me to delegate tasks and decisions much more effectively, both to my own personal betterment and to the overall improvement of the company as a whole.

Dr. Nick has made such a profound difference in my own life that I would highly recommend his services to anyone.

Short of his amazing expertise, however, I think that great improvements are possible to anyone who is willing to lead themselves through a similar examination. Within that process, I think the first place to begin the evaluation is—as I began this chapter—with the beginning.

I was taken aback—perhaps a little more than I should have been—by how the traits and characteristics I had developed as a child had come to shape my life as an adult. I am not unique in that respect, and so I would suggest that the first point of consideration should be just what part of the child in you continues to influence

I would suggest that the first point of consideration should be just what part of the child in you continues to influence your thoughts and actions as an adult.

your thoughts and actions as an adult.

Confronting this question is often more difficult in practice than it sounds, which brings me to another of Dr. Nick's helpful practices. There are few activities that an individual can engage in which produce a greater mental and physical benefit than developing a regular practice of meditation.

Dr. Nick encourages this not only in the more traditional sense of "clearing" one's mind, but also in his own "super-charged" version of meditation, which leads a practitioner to *fill* their minds with visions of both their performances and the triumphant outcomes of those activities they create in their minds. By running through that sequence of events over and over again, Dr. Nick has discovered a way to enable his patients to realize those same rewards in actuality. As Dr. Nick says, "If you believe it, you act it out."

And so, if the first step in the journey is to begin to take care of yourself in a wholesome and holistic way—and it is—then the place to start is at the very beginning:

Sit down and take an honest inventory of yourself, from your childhood to today: Identify the factors that interfere with your concentration; develop your resistance to stress; and follow a daily meditation and/or mindfulness practice.

4

Heal Thyself

t is inevitable that the top executives of any corporation will become intimately familiar and well-versed in the products and services that their organization brings to the market. That is, the top automakers know cars, the heads of Microsoft and Apple know computers.

No surprises there.

And so, I feel particularly blessed to be the captain of a company whose main product is health.

Loretto is a comprehensive, continuing healthcare organization that provides a variety of services for older adults and those adults who have special needs for ongoing care and treatment throughout Central New York.

We are, perhaps, best known throughout the industry for our compassionate philosophy and unique approach to providing such ongoing healthcare to our guests, most importantly by our concerted efforts at deinstitutionalizing our nursing homes and long-term care services and replacing them with home-like settings utilizing person-first care that emphasizes personal interaction.

I like to think that, even more than this, Loretto is really in the business of health and I truly believe that is simply a wonderful "product" to bring into the world.

On a personal level, my takeaway from the incredible opportunity I enjoy at Loretto has been a greater understanding of the value of that product, the importance of health—not just for those in our care, but for all of us.

Health. That's one of those items that people say quite frequently, but few of us ever take the time or opportunity to give the sort of deep thought and consideration that the prospect deserves.

So, do it right now. Take a moment and consider the value of your own health.

We live in a society today where the rush to achieve personally and professionally, the media's ceaseless mad chatter,

> Take a moment and consider the value of your own health.

and the unavoidable stressors to be found in even the most routine of daily activities can often leave us focused on less-important topics and nonsense, while ignoring the most essential of them all: our health.

If ignoring the importance of our heath or taking it for granted weren't bad enough, those societal and professional pressures often lead us into patterns of behavior that actually have the associated effect of compromising that most precious gift. There is an unfortunate, but prevailing, perception that corporate performance at an elite level requires that one adopt a lifestyle that is, at its foundation, unhealthy.

Skipping meals is often regarded as a demonstration of character, either as the fortitude to resist some edible temptation or as a demonstration of denial as dedication to one's career. Working through meals or "catching something at my desk" has become *de riguer* behavior of the young executive working his way up to the top—and the not-so-young ones who want to stay there.

Similarly, sleep deprivation is often lauded as a sign of constitutional strength or offered as an exhibit of "hard work." The ability to work through the night or appear for early mornings, to go consecutive days without any significant sleep, is considered as simply "paying the dues."

These perceptions, however, are entirely misguided. Dangerous.

The first step of the key tenet of Lifecircle Leadership—pragmatic altruism—must necessarily be getting in touch with yourself on an inner-personal basis, as Dr. Nick has guided me over the years. Certainly, that level of insight into my own psyche has allowed me to better understand my strengths. And weaknesses. And how to address both.

And through those efforts I have learned how to be kind to myself in a way that had escaped me for far too long. That demonstration of Lifecircle Leadership's pragmatic altruism within myself has opened my heart and my mind to a myriad of experiences that have afforded me the opportunity to grow in the most incredible ways.

It seems quite natural to me that the next step would be to address the physical self, to gain a similar understanding, and then to demonstrate an equal level of kindness and compassion. In other words, where we first practiced pragmatic altruism for the mind and soul, the next step becomes pragmatic altruism for the self.

The psyche and the physical self are, after all, tied to one another inextricably and what one does to one creates implications and effects within the other. An internal version of "So above, so below," if you will.

So, take, for example, an ambitious junior executive whom we can call Bill. Because he wants to demonstrate that he is committed to his job, he frequently skips lunch. Maybe works through dinner.

He lives on vending machine snacks or grabs a burger on his way home, or a cold plate of whatever's left in the fridge.

He thinks this demonstrates an exemplary level of commitment, but he couldn't be more mistaken. What that behavior evidences is a complete disregard for himself physically. And while his youth may sustain this sort of lifestyle for a period of time, very quickly those habits will begin to have an adverse effect on him. Whatever productivity he thinks he realizes in the time he steals from eating well will quickly be outbalanced by a lack of concentration from lowered blood sugar or other adverse mood reaction to the lack of nutritious food.

> The psyche and the physical self are, after all, tied to one another inextricably and what one does to one creates implications and effects within the other.

I can tell you with certainty that the literature in the health-care field leaves no doubt about the importance of maintaining a healthy diet. I offer this not as a tip for looking good on the beach or even as a way of guaranteeing a longer life. Rather, abundant evidence suggests that a healthy diet is necessary for the sort of optimal mental performance that is required of every young executive—and every employee, in general.

In the same way, Bill thinks his superiors will be impressed by his blurry-eyed estimations of just how long he's been working without a break. I certainly understand that there are times when the amount of work required to be completed in a compacted timeframe simply doesn't allow adequate time for sleep. And that's fine—once in a blue moon. Still, ample evidence indicates that lack of sleep quickly diminishes intellectual activity and emotional balance—both of them very necessary to the proper execution of any executive's duties.

As a result, Bill thinks he's putting in the time necessary to make a name for himself as a candidate for that next promotion or corporate opening, but all he's really accomplishing is making himself fuzzy-headed, irritable, and sick. His mental faculties will be increasingly diminished and—perhaps even more importantly—his emotions will become unbalanced. Neither one is an ideal state for performing at a level necessary to reach the corporate heights to which he aspires.

While there is an understandable temptation to deprive yourself of the basic necessities, such as food, sleep, etc., as you climb the corporate ladder, that sort of behavior only produces diminishing returns.

As with other aspects of practicing Lifecircle Leadership's pragmatic altruism, the key is to be kind; in this case, kind to yourself by furnishing yourself with all of the elements necessary to protect and serve your health.

And in keeping with that principle, the returns will be far greater than you could possibly expect.

5

The Workplace

The workplace in the era of The Impulse Society has become a devastatingly difficult place to survive, much less to thrive in any meaningful personal or professional manner. Technological advancements and seismic changes across industries have only increased the demands being made on all of us, from entry-level employees to those of us who occupy the corporate suites and corner offices.

One of the more disturbing developments is that there now exists a relentless and continuous sense of urgency (real or imagined) that demands almost immediate response to absolutely any issue that may be raised, no matter how or when it is advanced. I know plenty of executives whose personal lives and professional careers have been unwillingly merged into a single servitude to a steady stream of emails and texts that continue all hours of the day and night.

The perceived need to respond to each and every item that appears in one's inbox or flashes across the smartphone home screen is, I suppose, understandable, given that there is also a heightened level of visibility that accompanies most positions today, especially as it relates to perceived failures. We have forever lost that time when the majority of business was conducted with a significant level of privacy and discretion surrounding it. Today, the forum has changed, primarily because of social media's ever-increasing importance in business and our day-to-day lives. One of the unfortunate results of these developments is that there is now a disturbing level of voyeurism that pervades all aspects of corporate life, including the invariable failures. In a society that seems to be increasingly focused on the negative, the collective gaze is particularly focused on the failures.

These days, each executive misstep is sensationalized and dressed up as Internet click-bait, every corporate regime change is fair game for speculation, and every solicitous situation is played out in full public view. Accordingly, it should come as no surprise that executives naturally feel an increasing pressure from the scrutiny of being under the social microscope day in and day out.

Additionally, as the markets have changed and industries undergone shake-ups, there have been widespread restrictions on the resources available to many executives in the executions of their duties. With the heightened public scrutiny through social media and shareholders' increasing emphasis on market performance, the operational budgets of many companies have been cut to the bone in order to limit costs and pump up profits.

And, finally, given that much of our collective culture has been reduced to a series of clicks and swipes, it is not surprising that the attention span of much of the American public has been reduced to mere memes and sound-bites. Meaningful coverage of any news story doesn't ever expand past

> The attention span of much of the American public has been reduced to mere memes and sound-bites.

what's "hot" enough to open the morning shows. While the rapid decline of America's collective powers of concentration is regrettable for any number of reasons, the current climate does not make it any easier on executives and board directors to get their employees, colleagues, and shareholders to focus on important issues that require careful consideration.

The combined effects of these several conditions has been that many executives now find themselves in the unenviable position of being asked to produce immediate results with fewer resources, all while the entire world watches from the wings—many of them secretly hoping for some *schadenfreude*-inducing disaster captured on the Internet.

It's an impossible situation, but a perfect explanation for why so many of today's corporate executives feel overburdened and worn out. Numerous studies have reported that increasing numbers ever year of executives feel a serious degree of burnout.[14]

Unfortunately, for all too many of those beleaguered executives, working harder is the only reasonable solution that they see for their predicament. Of course, this approach does nothing to alleviate the stress and strain, but only accelerates the individual toward their eventual (and perhaps inevitable) breaking point.

It's not that a greater remedy doesn't exist. I have found that simple but remarkably effective steps can be taken to climb down off of the merry-go-round and reclaim a life lost to the gathering madness of the current corporate culture.

The first step is to simply take a deep breath and allow yourself the opportunity to thoroughly review a particular prompt before reacting to it in a knee-jerk fashion.

---

14   Harry Levinson, "When Executives Burn Out," *Harvard Business Review*, Aug. 21, 2014, hbr.org/1996/07/when-executives-burn-out.

The truth of the matter is that no one is ever at their best in a reactive state, which is a primitive and unrefined mind set. Today's corporate fast track requires calm, cool calculations and the instinctive response to complex issues is never a suitable course of action.

I have learned that there are very few situations that really require the sort of time-sensitive turnaround that the initiating party almost always demands. Moreover, I have likewise discovered that there are even fewer scenarios that require any sort of immediate response.

Taking a moment, taking that deep breath, will provide the opportunity to collect thoughts, regulate emotions, and thoughtfully examine whatever issue has been placed into action. I don't think it is possible to overemphasize the importance of this particular step. And by thoughtful examination, I mean not just the immediate situation but the foreseeable repercussions, as well. It is essential to analyze the short, medium, and long game at all times.

I can't count the number of times I have encountered an unfortunate (unpleasant) situation that arose primarily because someone responded without time for rational thought. Time and time again I have seen situations blow up over nothing because someone felt the need to respond to what was taken as some slight in an email they didn't read carefully or the perceived "tone" in a telephone call that started badly and got worse from there.

Once time has been taken, the next step for the executive is to decide whether the issue is actually within their respective decision-making circle or

> Time and time again I have seen situations blow up over nothing because someone felt the need to respond to what was taken as some slight in an email they didn't read carefully.

whether there is someone else within the organization who would be better suited to handle it.

As I've described elsewhere in these pages, when I assumed my role at Loretto, I felt an unhealthy compulsion to take on everything that everyone brought to me. Not only was this an exhausting process, but it taught me the hard lesson that once you assume a position of leadership, those under your supposed chain of command will immediately bring you items for action that are actually their own responsibility. The irony of the situation wasn't lost on me: Well-meaning leaders can usurp the work of their colleagues.

So, the next step is to create a well-defined hierarchy that creates zones of authority that are observed throughout the organization. That is, everyone has to understand their respective role, including the associated responsibilities and levels of authority.

When doing this, it is important not simply to make impersonal assignments and delegations of authority, but to utilize the creation of this hierarchy as an opportunity to build meaningful relationships. There was a time when employees were thought to respond to any command that was barked in their direction, but if those standards were ever effective (and I sincerely doubt that they ever worked), the time for those sorts of interactions is long past. Instead, meaningful relationships premised on mutual trust and loyalty are preferable.

Study after study has shown conclusively that this sort of trust-oriented leadership inspires personal loyalty and that it is this sort of loyalty, not necessarily any level of expertise, that is most indicative of employee reaction when the organization comes under fire.

Once that structure is in place, it is essential that everyone respect and observe them. Always. It is essential that they be followed consistently and without exception. Everybody works better in an environment that is grounded in certainty and routine. When the boundaries are clear and there is strict adherence to the same, the rest is easy. You need simply follow through.

The next time that an "urgent" email or text comes intruding into your day (or night), the response is simply to take a moment to breathe and consider it in full. Then decide whether the item properly falls within your area of authority or if it might be better handled by another member of the organization.

If the item falls within your bailiwick—handle it. If not, delegate it to the appropriate team member.

Simple. Effective. Lifesaving.

6

Leadership

O ne of the issues most often raised with me is the question of what makes a good leader. I think the answer is fairly simple and consistently applicable—at least within our system at Loretto—regardless of whether that leader is someone who is responsible for a shift of nurses or someone in my position with responsibility for thousands of employees and millions of dollars in revenue.

The first rule is simply to be yourself, to do what comes naturally.

At the same time, I think every manager has a responsibility to exercise a certain level of self-awareness and be aware of whatever toxicity they might be bringing into a situation. I think the easiest way to accomplish this is to look back at the negative examples of bosses that all of us have encountered over the course of our careers, from our very first jobs as kids to whatever position we might currently hold. All the bosses whom we have all struggled with

> The first rule is simply to be yourself, to do what comes naturally.

and disliked. The Yeller. The Micromanager. The Credit Thief.

Over the course of my career, I've had every one of those archetypes as a boss and I don't believe I'm alone in that regard. We are all familiar with each brand of this sort of negativity.

The first step to self-awareness is simply to exercise a bit of self-review to determine whether any of those negative qualities are present in your personal leadership style, and then to take measures to address them. That's the easy part. If you look in the mirror and recognize that you have negative qualities as a manager, just stop it.

The next step is to take those collective memories of your early positions and think of the manager you wish you had leading you during those formative years … and then be that boss.

For example, when I came aboard at Loretto, I was told that my predecessor never left his office, never got in the mix with employees either in terms of philanthropic activities or active problem solving or any of the other aspects that have been commonplace under my tenure. I am not criticizing that particular managerial style. I'm certainly not implying anything negative about that individual.

It was simply a matter that I knew what kind of manager I always wanted to work under and that wasn't an individual who was unapproachable. So, I made the effort to become the leader that I would have chosen to work for and I incorporated all of the attributes I wanted to project to become the boss that everyone has always wanted to work for.

I'm not saying that I have become the perfect boss. Far from it.

I'm simply saying that I have aspirations in that regard and that I am confident that my employees are aware of my efforts and appreciate them. More than that, I truly believe that they sense my desire to better myself on their behalf, and the vast majority of them reciprocate those sentiments, trying to better themselves as employees.

In this regard, the one point on which I might extend a word of caution is that whatever else a leader may be in terms of attentiveness or outgoingness or whatever other quality might come to mind, everything must be sincere and genuine or it will never work.

I say this not only because a disingenuous motive is always exposed in the end, but because it is simply too difficult to maintain a masquerade over an extended period of time—and being a leader is a 24/7/365 position.

That was something that took me a moment or two to realize when I first assumed a leadership role at Loretto, but I quickly came to the understanding that my behavior had to be reflective of the role I was in at all times. I had to be mindful of my words and behavior because I came to realize that people were always watching. That's just how it is.

> I quickly came to the understanding that my behavior had to be reflective of the role I was in at all times.

That's a big responsibility, being the last stop on the train. When you assume that position, everything you say and do has weight and meaning to it. And because of that you can never fall back to a reactive position because it's a 24/7/365 accessibility and visibility of your life, almost in the same way as it was for actors and politicians in the past. These days, because technology is so ubiquitous, there is an expectation that you are "on" at all times.

As a result, it is imperative that your leadership style provides an honest and true reflection of your real face, your most sincere, best self.

That's the importance of working on yourself, not just to improve your own personal experience, but to prepare yourself for the leadership role ahead of you—whether that position is one that you currently occupy or one which you seek to occupy in the future.

While I suppose there are as many styles of leadership as there are individuals, we are really considering three primary philosophical schools of thought on the subject.

The first of these is a *transformational* style of leadership, so called because it "transforms" followers by engaging their emotions, values, ethics, and motivations in pursuit of a long-term goal. This is, obviously, a highly personal means of establishing leadership by building personal relationships. This is the particular style that works best for me and is most in line with my natural personality.

The second school is known as *authentic* leadership. I find this style more personally reserved, where leaders following this path would demonstrate a strong sense of their purpose in life, their core values, and their perceptions of the "right" thing to do. By demonstrating self-discipline and acting on those strongly held values, they establish trusting relationships, but not necessarily friendships. I think the philosophical school that would be closest would be Stoicism and, for that reason, I have always found this particular style to be very masculine in its nature.

The third style is *servant* leadership, and (exactly as that sounds) it is premised on the leader clearly establishing that the primary objective is the service of others, before the satisfaction of personal goals and desires.

There is no right style of leadership and, I think, most people would find that what works best is some combination of two or three, depending upon one's own personality traits, specific workplace situations, and the respective personalities of the employees or individuals one seeks to lead. In that regard, I think it is good and natural to maintain a level of consistency in one's leadership style, but still have the flexibility necessary to adapt to whatever situation might present itself. Oftentimes, the most significant difference between leaders with average influence and those leaders with great influence is nothing more than adaptability and behavior flexibility.[15]

Similarly, I think it's important to keep in mind that one's leadership style is—like every other component of a greater personality—something that must undergo growth and evolution over time. For that reason, I think the most important element is simply that one makes a determined effort to consider and develop their leadership style with conscious intention of becoming the best leader possible.

I recognize that that might seem like a foregone conclusion, but I don't believe that it is. Back to my earlier suggestion to consider all of the leaders whom you might have had over the course of your career, I think most of us would have memories of more than a few bosses who clearly gave no thought whatsoever to their leadership style. And, for that reason, I think the most important element is simply a sincere desire to be the best leader possible.

---

15   Rebecca Newton, "What Great Leaders Know About Influence," *Forbes Magazine*, Aug. 2, 2016, www.forbes.com/sites/rebeccanewton/2016/07/27/six-steps-to-increase-your-influence/#26de27fa1edd.

7

Establish a Hierarchy, and Listen

While I have laid out the basics of Lifecircle Leadership, I think there are some elements that deserve a bit closer examination: construction of a hierarchy, for example.

I have already made clear that I am not by nature a person who can take full advantage of a hierarchy situation. I think my lacking in this regard stems from the fact that for so much of my professional life I was completely responsible for pursuing and attaining my own goals without the advantage of anyone reliable in my life to whom I might delegate some of those tasks.

Moreover, I have always been a person who believes that there are two ways of doing anything: the right way and the wrong way.

I have an innate knowledge about how things should be done and often those views demand a significant amount of more detail and attention than many people are willing to commit. As a result, I have learned that if I want something to be done the right way, it is often necessary—or, at least, easier—for me to take on whatever the task may be by myself.

I plead guilty. *Mea culpa.*

But I'm hardly alone in dealing with a natural reluctance to trust the system and participate fully in a cooperative approach to achieving objectives within the workspace.

In fact, I think this situation is extremely common and widespread throughout all strata of corporate America, if it's not the existing standard. And I think the reasons for that are many—and completely understandable.

If the American workplace, particularly the upper-echelons of corporate activity, were ever a forgiving environment (and I don't think that they ever were), then today's models have erased whatever modicum of understanding and forbearance that might have once existed—even if that "benefit of the doubt" was only the old boy network watching out for its own.

The truth of the matter is that in today's uber-competitive corporate culture, there is little room for forgiveness and one wrong outcome can spell disaster for—even end—a career. Accordingly, there's no great mystery as to why those involved in that particular process feel more compelled than ever to ensure that everything is done the "right way," even if that means doing everything themselves.

On the flip end of the coin, where capitalism on a whole is premised philosophically on the advantages to be gained from healthy

> The truth of the matter is that in today's uber-competitive corporate culture, there is little room for forgiveness and one wrong outcome can spell disaster for—even end—a career.

(and unhealthy) competition and corporate environments often intensify those struggles to create a sort of inner-office gladiatorial contest, people often feel the need to take on even the most formidable tasks by themselves, thinking that the involvement of others will dilute the glory to be gained in the completion or offer an opportunity for some inner-office *Game of Thrones* treachery to steal the credit—and whatever rewards may be attached.

I certainly understand these positions and the culture that makes them so prevalent in our workplaces, but that does nothing to address the toxicity that they are breeding within our organizations and within our relationships with our coworkers.

The fact is that good leaders create situational opportunities for those under their direction and that this necessarily involves creating a hierarchy that not only improves the emotional conditions of the workplace, but also the efficiency and potency of the organization itself.

I think it's understandable, particularly for someone new to a position of leadership, that you think you have to have every answer for every problem and situation. But that's simply not the case.

Very early in my corporate tenure, I learned that I needed to create a hierarchy—not only to lessen my own burden to something that was humanly possible, but to include the valuable talents and experiences of those who were working with me.

I learned that the most important aspect of a hierarchy is simply clarity. Everyone needs (and wants) to know what lane they're to swim in. People don't do well when there's uncertainty about their authority or their tasks or their areas of responsibility. And so, it is essential that everyone involved in the process be absolutely aware of the parameters of their respective positions—and this requires complete clarity from the leadership.

As a result, when I was confronted with a situation, I was able to take a little more time to consider whose responsibility this situation actually was and not rely on my old knee-jerk reaction of assuming the responsibility myself. I realized that not every decision was necessarily my decision.

And I certainly learned that there are, in actuality, very few items that demand an immediate response. To the contrary, getting as much collective information as you can on the front end so that you can make the best overall decision is infinitely more important that simply reacting quickly.

This, in turn, led to the conclusion that I probably didn't have all the answers anyway. I likely had a *piece* of the answer, but I was surrounded by capable colleagues who also had pieces of a more complete and better answer. I resisted the toxic compulsion of *The Impulse Society*, that every issue demanded an immediate response and/or solution and took the time to create a dialogue within the clearly marked zones of authority that I had created.

That dialogue is the second component of improving decision making and overall performance, from the patient floors to the board rooms. Opening a direct line of communications is essential.

One of the first measures I took when I assumed the leadership at Loretto was to establish a policy of open communications, not only between my fellow executives but also with absolutely everyone who is a part of the Loretto organization—and, I would say, family.

I took the time to set up open discussion groups with every facility. I met with people in administration and nurses and nurses' aides. I met and talked with everybody that I could. I would go all over the Loretto system and show up at places, convene people, and would say, "I don't

> Opening a direct line of communications is essential.

have an agenda. This is a listening session. I'm here to listen and answer questions. If I know the answer, I'll tell you honestly. If I don't know, I'll find the appropriate party who does. But I want to talk to you because what you have to say matters to me."

The results of that endeavor were absolutely incredible to me.

Initially, I was met with a certain (not entirely unexpected) reserve and reluctance to engage in this dialogue. This was true across the board; some of my highest colleagues and the newest hires all had their suspicions about opening their mouths and engaging in an open and free conversation with someone that they regarded as "The Big Boss."

I persisted, because I knew it was important.

Once people became comfortable with the idea, once they learned to trust me, the conversations that came out of these meetings offered me an invaluable insight into my organization that I never would have been able to gain otherwise.

And that's what it was, really: a conversation with my organization.

There is a tendency, particularly for those of us who hold sets of corporate powers, to regard our organizations as something inanimate. That view, however, is dangerously inaccurate and limited.

Every corporation, no matter its relative size or earnings or position within the market, is a living and breathing entity, comprised by each and every human being who shows up each day to do their part on its behalf.

Humanizing Loretto in this way and beginning to talk about what was happening within the organization was maybe the single-most important step I've taken as president/CEO. I say this because I now understand Loretto not just from the balance sheets and performance reports that come across my desk, but in a deeper way from the relationships that I have been able to forge.

That insight and that connection have offered rewards enough to justify my efforts, but there have been even greater results.

To those who have never considered taking such step, I cannot say enough about the effects I have seen from simply telling everyone under my direction—and I mean *everyone*—that what you have to say matters to me. That spirit of inclusion has proven to work miracles across the board with our employees.

The results have been so significant that it amazes me that the practice is not more widespread. The initiative didn't add anything to our budget, didn't require any additional personnel or improvements.

It was simply a matter of taking the opportunity to tell everyone in my organization, "What you have to say matters to me. You matter to me."

The reaction of my employees to this has been tremendous.

There are volumes and volumes written on means and methods for inspiring your workforce and I think there is likely value in each and every piece written, but I think there is an even easier and more reliable alternative: simply tell your employees that you're listening.

And then show them you are.

8

A Tale of Two Americas

As I've mentioned previously, the book you now hold in your hands was the product of a good deal of evolution and development from my original intentions.

When I started the process, I was fixed on writing something that would address the concerns and potentials of C-level executives and those in upper-management who might harbor aspirations of attaining a corporate position on that elevated level. It was, admittedly, a restricted and rarified readership that I sought to address.

As the writing (and rewriting) process progressed, however, the focus of my work began to drift away from those with whom I shared the executive suite and migrated out into our operations as I became increasingly concerned with all of my employees.

As my focus expended, so too did the audience that I wanted to attract and address. I never surrendered the idea of communicating my ideas directly to a readership of corporate and legal professionals at a very high level, but I found more and more that I wanted to make my message(s) applicable to and accessible for everyone.

I soon found, however, that there was a significant obstacle in coursing this objective: there is a divide between these two respective potential readerships. Even more concerning, we find ourselves at a particularly perilous time in which the communications between these two relative camps has never been more polarizing and counterproductive.

And so, what to do?

I took a good deal of inspiration from Charles Dickens's classic *A Tale of Two Cities*. The most obvious interpretation of that title is, of course, a quite literal one that focuses on the simple fact that the novel's action is literally split in part between two cities: Paris and London.

I have always believed, however, that Dickens was far subtler with his title, and wrote of the more complex socio-economic dualities of both of those particular cities in the historical period just before the French Revolution.

There is one city (Paris or London, it is the same for both) for the affluent and socio-politically well-connected, and another altogether for those without money and privilege. That is, even those characters who share a common location know a much different city based entirely upon their status and affluence.

In the very same way that Dickens identified this dichotomy in Europe during the eighteenth century, I believe there is no question that we live in two Americas here in the twenty-first century—and perhaps we always have.

One America exists within the privileged bubble of those who are fortunate enough to afford the pleasures and protections that are offered beneath its dome. The other exists in a much harsher reality, in which poverty and political disenfranchisement create an environment that is difficult (some might reasonably argue *impossible*) to escape and contains jeopardy and consequences at every juncture.

In the same way, while I certainly have a strong moral compass that inclines me to view this situation through a filter of compassion,

I have likewise restrained myself from applying this to the arguments I am advancing herein.

There are two Americas. One for those who are financially comfortable. Another for those who are not. The duality of America is simply a fact. There is a diverse and broad spectrum of life experiences out there—I think we all benefit from accepting and embracing them all.

And that, in and of itself, may be the most important lesson that I would wish to convey.

When I first came to Loretto, I instituted a practice of sitting down with my employees. All of them.

> There is a diverse and broad spectrum of life experiences out there—I think we all benefit from accepting and embracing them all.

I would schedule time to sit down with my fellow executives and discuss their concerns.

And then I would ask for the opportunity to do the same with those who staffed our day-to-day operations.

More than a few people (from both sides) suggested I was being naïve or wasting my time—even worse, wasting theirs. But I believed adamantly that, particularly in my first years at the head of the company, one of the most important things that I could do was to simply listen and learn.

And time and time again, that has proven to be true.

I repeatedly read articles advancing the theory that there is a discernible decline in the level of empathy that we have collectively for our fellow human beings. Certainly, a review of news stories or ten minutes in front of a TV support this suggest of a growing lack of compassion, but I don't believe this is the same as saying that we, as a society, have developed a callous heart.

I don't think the prevalent problem is that people don't care. I think the true issue isn't that they lack compassion, so much as it is that they lack understanding. It's not necessarily that we as a society have grown indifferent to the suffering of others, but that we have become so isolated that we no longer have knowledge of that suffering. We simply don't have a great enough understanding of other's lives to be empathetic.

> It's not necessarily that we as a society have grown indifferent to the suffering of others, but that we have become so isolated that we know longer have knowledge of that suffering.

Allow me to take you back to the pre-Revolution France that Dickens brought to life in that novel of his. One of the most (in)famous quotes of that historical era is attributed to Marie Antoinette who, when told that her people were starving so terribly that they didn't even have bread, then supposedly remarked, "Let them eat cake."

It seems, of course, to be a terribly cold and wicked comment to make in the face of widespread starvation. It was so shocking as to become a flashpoint for the Revolution and that is exactly how the comment has been remembered and regarded over the ages since then.

While many historians dispute whether Marie Antoinette said the infamous words at all, almost all agree that the famous quote of hers was taken completely out of context. Rather than reflecting a wicked disregard for human suffering, her words were merely the product of her own cultural disconnect from the majority of her people.

The current historical consensus suggests that Marie was raised in such luxury that her own table was always overflowing with food, including bread—and cakes. Lots of cakes.

Having never experienced anything but an overabundance of food, poor Marie was simply culturally unable to conceive that anyone else's experience might differ from her own and so she innocently offered what she must have thought was a common-sense solution. If there wasn't any bread on the table, simply "let them eat cake."

In the same way, I think we currently find ourselves in a situation in which we are not necessarily indifferent to the adversity of others, but merely lack an understanding of it.

Opening the dialogue and accepting what we learn from that exchange is the first—and very necessary—step.

9

Every Little Bit Helps

Here's a perfect example of the problems that are significant in one America and non-existent in the other: diapers.

Yes, you read that right, diapers. Paper underpants for babies.

When I initiated my practice of going out into the various facilities that Loretto operates and talking to the people who put in the shifts day-to-day, one of the first facts that I came away with was that diapers were far more important than I had ever imagined—and I have six kids, so I know my way around a diaper.

> Based largely on the dialogue that was opened during those employee chat sessions, I took the initiative to introduce a new program throughout our operations.

Based largely on the dialogue that was opened during those employee chat sessions, I took the initiative to introduce a new program throughout our operations. We would establish a "diaper bank," a repository of the items, and would distribute a set number to those workers who expressed a need to receive them.

Many of my (male) executives greeted the announcement of the program with a grin. Some others overlooked the humor that was evidently to be found in such a practice and instead questioned the soundness of Loretto giving anything away to our employees.

The reaction was not unexpected and, I suppose, not entirely unreasonable either. Marie Antoinette, right?

Let me introduce you to Lila. Lila is a nurse's assistant, a fine one. Her supervisors have identified her as smart, compassionate, and committed. They all have great confidence that under the right circumstances, Lila could develop her skills and advance in her profession.

The events of that scenario would greatly improve Lila's life.

From my own perspective, developing her skills and advancing her through Loretto's own ranks would be a great benefit to our own interests. There is just one problem. Not really a problem, but more an issue: Lila is a single mother with two children, ages two years and four months.

While her children are the most important thing in Lila's life and, quite frankly, the reason that she gets up every morning and works so hard at Loretto every day, they do create a responsibility and their care often vies with her work obligations.

Of course, that concern is significantly lightened by the daycare she has the kids enrolled in, but guess what? That's right, diapers.

First, let's understand that these things are expensive. I only point this out (and describe just how expensive below) because a significant number of the executives and professionals I deal with everyday have never bought a box of diapers or didn't pay attention to the price if they did. But so that they can understand just what Lila is up against, allow me to break down the numbers. A box of a hundred or so will run upwards of thirty dollars.

And for Lila, who has limited access to discount shopping in those areas that require a car to reach, she's dependent upon smaller, "neighborhood" stores in which items are routinely significantly more expensive than at other retailers.

The average child goes through about ten diapers a day. So, for Lila, with two children, that means she needs twenty diapers a day. Work that out, that means that the hundred-count box of diapers will last her about five days (and we'll ignore for a moment that children of different ages and sizes require different sized diapers).

That's six boxes a month, or $180.00. That's a staggering amount for a single mother of two to factor into her monthly budget before even considering any of the other most basic necessities for her and her family.

Returning to our original scenario, however, because diapers are so prohibitively expensive, most daycare centers—and certainly all of the facilities servicing a lower-income clientele—do not provide diapers for the children in their care. Instead, these facilities demand that parents leave a deposit of diapers with them to ensure that there will be a sufficient supply. Without maintaining that supply of diapers, however, the daycare centers will not accept the child into their care. More often than not, this is not a request or a lip service policy, it's a hard, no-exceptions-please demand.

If a child does not have a reserve of diapers each and every day, then they are simply not permitted to attend the day care until the necessary personal supply is replenished. Simply put: no diapers, no daycare.

As a result, if Lila can't afford to provide diapers to her children's daycare, then she can't leave them there under their care. And, with no one else that she can trust to care for her children, that means that she can't show for her shift. She loses a day's pay.

And so, while $180 is absolutely a seemingly insurmountable burden for a single mother of two to meet before she has put a roof over her family's heads, fed them, or provided basic utilities, her capacity to meet those obligations is compromised by a day's wages simply because of the financial burden. In the end, it all becomes a devastating cycle of financial disaster.

And the economic loses aren't Lila's alone.

Loretto loses a fine employee and incurs the bother and expense of getting someone else to cover that missed shift. And those costs—while they may appear minimal when considered as a single, isolated event—become significant over time when they are applied to repeated events and multiple employees. All of that over a couple of diapers.

So, I decided that Loretto would create its own Diaper Bank. We amassed a supply of diapers and administered it so fifty free diapers per child per month were distributed to every employee who, like Lila, demonstrated a need to participate in the program. Once enrolled, Lila and the other employees in her position, receive diapers that they can provide to their day care center in order to ensure the continued care of their children. And this enables her to meet all of her assigned shifts at Loretto.

The results for Lila and the other employees like her have been nothing short of amazing. Not only do these employees who once lost a day's wages here or there on a fairly regular basis now have an uninterrupted income stream, but the work they perform is equally improved. Without these concerns about who will take care of their children and with the financial burden of providing for their families lightened, these employees perform their job-related duties much better than they previously had.

A Diaper Bank seemed a minor accommodation to many when

the program began. Admittedly, the program was limited in its intended scope. And, honestly, I was never offended by those who smirked at my proposal. I always understood that those who had never been in Lila's position might not understand.

The fact remains, however, that this limited program and its minor accommodations made a significant difference in Lila's life and the lives of many other Loretto employees—and their children.

It made a difference for Loretto, as well.

As such, our Diaper Bank stands as proven example of the wonderful repercussions that are created by even the smallest act of kindness.

With that shining example, the question then becomes what more can be done? At Loretto. Within your own organization.

If you were to sit down and listen to what your employees need, not only in the performance of their professional duties, but in the overall context of their lives, what would they reveal they need?

And then, what would addressing those needs cost?

> If you were to sit down and listen to what your employees need, not only in the performance of their professional duties, but in the overall context of their lives, what would they reveal they need?

What benefits would be returned in exchange?

This is a simple conversation, but one which can be incredibly rewarding to all of those who are willing to participate and who will remember that even the littlest gestures can have enormous returns.

10

Community

n the same way that our efforts within Loretto are intended to address the needs of those who were the most at risk within our workplace, similar gestures will bear similar results beyond the confines when applied to the community at large.

Community.

While there have certainly been important advancements made in the twenty-first century, I can't help but lament the loss of some of the elements of the twentieth century. Today, *community* is a geo-political phrase; something they teach in Human Geography classes. But that's only its current meaning.

There was a time when community meant something more, when it called out a group of people not only living and working in proximity to one another, but also actively sharing the lives that they led there. That time has passed—for now.

My community is Syracuse, New York. While Syracuse currently has the unfortunate distinction of being one of the most impover-ished cities in the United States, there was a time when circumstances were considerably different. There was a time when Syracuse wasn't any different from the rest of the country, basking in the prosperity of post-WWII America.

General Electric had a significant presence here—Carrier Corporation, too. There was industry here and good jobs. The community built itself around those opportunities. And during this period, Syracuse was the capital center of the entire Upstate New York region. Universities were established and thrived. I would later come to call it my alma matter.

Ethnic enclaves were established. Neighborhoods. Communities. And by that, I mean people who cared for one another. But times change, and Syracuse changed with them. The GE plant closed, as then did Carrier. And like so many other cities around the country, the money went with them.

Today, the universities remain, but there is little else to remind one of the brighter days in Syracuse's past.

As I've discussed, poverty has replaced prosperity and a sense of abandonment now permeates the same neighborhoods that were once rich with a spirit of community. As with any other area in which there is an unusually high density of poverty, you will also find all of those (in)human conditions that almost always accompany such adversity: healthcare issues, educational issues, crime, and drugs.

> There are many living among this hardship who make daily demonstrations of their inner light, their indomitable spirit, and their refusal to compromise their dignity.

And at the same time, there are many living among this hardship who make daily demonstrations of their inner light, their indomitable spirit, and their refusal to compromise their dignity.

Many of these people are the same wonderful individuals who make up so much of the workforce at Loretto: Single moms. The undereducated and disenfranchised. Individuals who face seemingly insurmountable obstacles in their daily lives and yet, somehow, continue to persevere and do their jobs so they can serve their clients with compassion.

They are my motivation, not only in the execution of my duties at Loretto as the individual responsible for their continued employment and well-being, but also in my efforts to go above and beyond those traditional (and limited) corporate duties.

What I have done, as a result, is to lead Loretto into a series of relationships with an assortment of philanthropic groups and community organizers. I am aware that there are many within the corporate sphere who have looked askance at my efforts, perhaps even dismissed them as naïve or Pollyannaish.

I assure you that they are nothing of the sort.

To the contrary, I have put my basic philosophy of pragmatic altruism into practice in real-world situations and time-after-time the results have supported my contention that if we are able to act in the interest of the collective good, then there are very personal rewards that become available to all of us.

Moreover, the Lifecircle Leadership principle is universal and not restricted to personal actions. By putting Loretto—a multi-million-dollar entity on this very particular path, I have not only made significant improvements in the lives of my employees and the standards of the surrounding communities, but also created situations and relationships that have proved to offer real world benefits.

Pragmatic altruism is real. It works. And I have a number of examples to share with you.

11

The Train

t wasn't until I assumed my position as president/CEO of Loretto that I began to give any real thought to the cost of employment. For most people—and I would certainly include myself in their number at one time—the cost of employment seems to consist entirely of the wages paid an employee, together with the costs of any other benefits. Period.

I wish it were that simple.

Once you begin to examine the situation from a managerial perspective, you begin to understand all of the many unseen costs that must necessarily be factored into maintaining a work force.

To begin with, there is a cost involved in simply mounting and maintaining a hiring process. Many unsuccessful job applicants react bitterly at the thought that

> Once you begin to examine the situation from a managerial perspective, you begin to understand all of the many unseen costs that must necessarily be factored into maintaining a work force.

their resume was not studied or that their efforts did not elicit an interview opportunity, and yet they never give any consideration to the fact that there is a real cost associated with reviewing all of those resumes and applications. Those costs increase significantly when the process moves up the chain to an interview process.

Even the successful candidate fails to consider that the hiring itself carries with it many associated costs. And while I understand these elements might escape the consideration of the job applicant, I am always a bit taken aback when I realize how little thought many employers and managers give to the prospect.

The fact remains that the hiring process is an expensive endeavor. At Loretto, we estimate that we expend approximately $4,000 for each person hired.

Moreover, the costs do not dissipate significantly once the candidate is hired and integrated into the workforce. Again, I'm not referring solely to compensation and benefits.

There are costs associated with absenteeism, both actual failure to show to work and the sort of on-the-job absenteeism that has become increasingly problematic in workplaces across the country and at all levels (i.e., employees show up but are not engaged with their work). There are costs associated with staffing those missed shifts and assignments. And the costs continue to mount when there are disciplinary actions necessary or employment is terminated.

Certainly, maintaining a Human Resources department that can keep up with the increasingly complicated and numerous employment regulations, particularly in these times of unparalleled-social-sensitivity and hyper-litigiousness, is a significant expense, as well. Failure to do so can be disastrously expensive. All of these are just some of the components that go into the significant costs associated with the workforce.

In the same way, people frequently look at unemployment without fully considering the associated expenses. The sympathetic typically think in terms of more human costs, and the less than sympathetic center their complaints on actual dollars spent on benefits.

The costs, however, are significantly higher, both in a human and fiscal sense. Unemployment has a devastating impact on entire communities. I have certainly witnessed this in my experiences trying to improve conditions in Onondaga County, New York. Unemployment creates conditions that are fertile ground for criminal activity, which, in turn, is associated with increased costs of law enforcement, judicial system, and ultimately the penal system, as well.

Likewise, unemployment takes a devastating toll on overall health of all of the individuals impacted, which places greater demands on the public health system. More costs. Unemployment undermines family structures, making it less likely that children will perform well in school, which in turn continues to contribute to more unemployment.

So, there it is: Hiring and maintaining a workforce is a significant cost to private companies. Unemployment creates significant expenses for communities. Now what would you say if we could address both of those issues simultaneously through our use of pragmatic altruism?

We can.

I know, beyond a shadow of a doubt, because Loretto is one of a handful of companies that is on the forefront of an exciting new program designed to address both of these issues.

> Now what would you say if we could address both of those issues simultaneously through our use of pragmatic altruism? We can.

Dominic Robinson is the vice president of economic inclusion for the CenterState Corporation for Economic Opportunity and the innovator behind a bold new initiative called WorkTrain.

Unemployment is certainly a serious problem throughout Upstate New York. According to statistics from the New York State Department of Labor, unemployment in Onondaga County hovers at around 6 percent, with the rates of joblessness climbing above 8 percent in the counties to the north.[16] All of this against a national rate that is currently in the range of 4 percent.

That means that Onondaga County's unemployment rate is 50 percent greater than the national average and the counties to the north an alarming 100 percent higher.

In the midst of these distressing figures, however, what many fail to acknowledge is the significant percentage of individuals who are considered effectively "unemployable." That is, they lack certain fundamental skills or have certain qualities or characteristics that—although not often discussed in polite (or litigation-conscious) public—make it extremely unlikely that they will ever find meaningful employment or, in the odd event that they do, maintain that position for any length of time. What even those depressing facts and figures don't accurately portray is that among those numbers of the unemployed is another, sadder subset of the unemployable.

These are the individuals that Dominic wanted to reach out to with his WorkTrain initiative. The theory behind the program was simple enough: Take to hiring with a targeted approach to the specific needs of area employers. Approach vocational centers with the intent of letting all the candidates know that there was a fundamental belief that everyone has worth and is deserving of the opportunities and

---

16   "Local Area Unemployment Statistic Program," New York State Department of Labor, https://labor.ny.gov/stats/laus.asp.

support necessary to be successful.

Dominic and his staff assessed the employment needs of the first participants of the WorkTrain program. They discussed the skillsets that employers needed to incorporate into their operations and, more than that, they discussed the characteristics and qualities that made for an ideal employee.

Incorporating the insight gained from those conversations, Dominic and the folks at WorkTrain then turned to those in the community who were in need of employment and—most important of all—were willing to undergo the rigorous training necessary to transform them from the unemployable to the model employee.

The initial course of orientation and education for the first collection of candidates was rigorous. Over the course of three weeks, these individuals were tutored and trained not only in the specific skills that employers had identified were most essential to their operations, but also in developing those skills that would make them ideal employees and would enable them to actively contribute in a position of employment in the long haul—a new and original concept for many of the participants.

And then the hiring began and the test candidates were put to the challenge of the work-a-day world.

Almost without exception, the individuals who had successfully participated in and graduated from the WorkTrain program demonstrated in their performance that with the proper training and the right kind of support, those who had previously been considered to be "unemployable" could, in fact, be transformed into employees that far exceeded any reasonable expectations of an employer.

I have the great privilege of serving on the board of directors of United Way and so I was excited and intrigued to learn about the unqualified success of WorkTrain.

I was also a little jealous. As I've said, while most people might not ordinarily consider the costs involved in hiring, training, and maintaining an employee, as a corporate CEO, I am all too familiar with those facts and figures.

So I turned to Dominic with a single question: Could he do for Loretto everything that he achieved for other participating employers? The answer was HealthTrain.

The principle behind the Loretto program was exactly the same: take those members of the community who were largely disregarded as employee candidates and groom them for employment. This time, however, the specifics of their vocational training related to the health-care industry.

Again, training sessions of approximately three weeks were set up for prospective candidates and they were run through a process similar to what had been utilized during the WorkTrain initiatives. When the program was completed, the graduating candidates were interviewed by several area health-care providers, including Loretto.

The success of WorkTrain came to me in the form of enthusiastic reviews of participating employers and the reports that were made available to members of the board. The triumphs of Health-Train were different, however; those I had the privilege of witnessing up-close and on a very personal basis.

To begin with, the hiring process through HealthTrain was infinitely more streamlined, effective, and cost-efficient in reaching the unemployed than any that we could have mounted through our own Human Resources department and the usual source of candidates (i.e., advertisements, recruiters, etc.).

More importantly, the employee acquisitions that we made through the program have all, almost without exception, demonstrated themselves to be extraordinarily qualified and well-suited employees.

To that point, the figure that I am most proud of is our rate of retention. Currently, those who are brought into Loretto through HealthTrain enjoy a retention rate of more than 80 percent. In any industry, that would be a significant return, but in our corner of the market in which the emotional and physical toll of the ordinary performance of one's job are often beyond reasonable expectations, that sort of retention is nothing short of miraculous.

> Currently, those who are brought into Loretto through HealthTrain enjoy a retention rate of more than 80 percent.

All of this has created the most wonderful synergy imaginable.

Through our partnership with HealthTrain, I am proud of the number of individuals who previously held very little hope of ever finding meaningful, lasting employment who are now enjoying careers that provide them a living wage and the sort of benefits that they otherwise could not have known.

There is little question that these individuals have been transformed not only in terms of their employability, but also with regard to their personal self-esteem and the contributions they are now capable of making of making to their families, their communities, and to the region.

I have seen the transformations, not just in the balance sheets or reports, but in the smiles and bright eyes of the employees I am proud to greet every morning and work with side-by side every day.

I am also proud to report that the success of Dominic's projects, both WorkTrain and HealthTrain, has made the news and garnered the attention that it well deserves. There are employers throughout the region that have learned of the exceptional success that have been generated through the program and they are all understandably eager to participate in future generations of the program.

To my mind, this may best illustrate the principles of pragmatic altruism in action in the real world. There is no doubt that the spark to the creation of this program was the kindness and compassion in Dominic's heart and the hearts of all of those who worked so hard to bring this wonderful idea to real-world fruition.

It would not be fitting, however, to describe the program as charitable. Nothing has been given away, there is none of the "free lunch" generosity that for some reason seems to draw so much derision from some quarters in corporate America.

Instead, this is a program that has absolutely demonstrated the soundness of its implementation in real-world ways that any capitalist could appreciate and embrace. This is compassion that improves the corporate bottom line. And it improves human lives at the same time.

The perfect combination.

Those who have worked with the WorkTrain/HealthTrain programs—including myself—can see clearly that programs like these are the future, not only in hiring and training candidates, but in treating and relating to those in our society who may need a little extra guidance and support before they can be counted on to make the same sort of contributions that we collectively expect of some others.

And that's really what all of this is about, the understanding that there are some of us who may need a little extra assistance along the way, and that providing it to them, taking care of those among us who need it most, is not an act of superiority but of rational business decision making.

We are, all of us, interconnected and

In the end, how we take care of one another is how we are taken care of.

dependent upon each other. In the end, how we take care of one another is how we are taken care of. And when the chance to work for success is extended to those who have traditionally been denied those opportunities, their achievement yields rewards for all of us.

12

The First Step Is
Not Walking

While these programs are important, they do not represent a singular solution to the complex problems facing our community.

Despite the best interests of so many good people like Dominic Robinson, even securing a steady position of employment is no guarantee for the poorest among us. They can realize the sort of positive life experience so many of us take completely for granted.

And at the very heart of that life is a car. The United States is, after all, the ultimate car culture and it would be difficult (impossible?) for many of us to contemplate life without the use of a reliable automobile. We drive everywhere and many of our cities and communities are structured with that

> They can realize the sort of positive life experience so many of us take completely for granted.

mobility in mind, with many of the societal benefits that they offer available only to those who can drive to a certain location to take advantage of them.

This includes, for far more people than many might expect, employment.

At this point, I can already anticipate the responses of those who will point out that in many communities—primarily, metropolitan city centers—there are public transportation options that can be utilized to address some of those issues.

While that assortment is unquestionably true—at least, on the surface—it does not address the full scope of the inherent difficulties. Even worse, I fear it betrays a certain sort of unwitting cultural bias.

True, there is public transit available in many of the more urbanized areas of our country, but no one who has ever relied upon these services and shown up twenty minutes late for work because of a delay on the route or missed the last connection for the night will suggest that they can be regarded as reasonable alternative for a personal vehicle. And it's important to stress here that by this I mean not the sheer pleasure or convenience, but for the near necessity of reliable and safe personal transportation.

Again, let us consider the proposition by examining not the broad socio-economic debate, but the experience of a single individual caught in this seeming inescapable trap.

Linda is a nursing assistant at Loretto. She has worked with us for several years and over that time has demonstrated her capacity for the job and compassion for those in her care. She would make an excellent home health assistant, travelling throughout the community delivering those same services and compassion to those who do not reside in a facility but still require regular medical attention in their own living environments.

The promotion would represent a significant professional advancement for her and would bring a commiserate increase in her salary. There's just one problem: Linda doesn't have access to a car. That means that despite her talents and heart, she doesn't have the most necessary requirement for the job and she can't be advanced.

But Linda's situation is worse than that.

Because Linda has no car and is dependent upon the bus system to get to work, she is unfortunately reliant on their performance. If there is a delay in the line and the buses are running late, then Linda will likely miss one of her necessary connections or arrive at work after the start of her shift.

And if the demands of her work day are such that there remain patients in need of care even after her scheduled hours or if one of her coworkers has unexpectedly called off of their shift, Linda is unable to stay late and work the overtime because she needs to keep the bus company's strict schedule. This means that she is unable to take fullest advantage of the economic opportunities that might otherwise be available to her. For a woman in Linda's economic position, the promise of regular overtime and/or extra shifts is an important advantage in navigating the difficult financial straits of her circumstances.

Additionally, I think it's important at this juncture to look past the mere economic considerations to note here that using the public transportation systems—waiting for buses, walking to and from stops—particularly in the later hours, subjects a woman to a heightened level of personal vulnerability that also must be considered and factored into the situation.

Again, Linda is not the only entity who bears the burden of this less-than-perfect arrangement.

Linda's inability to take advantage of the opening as a home health assistant means that Loretto will once again be required to engage in the costly and burdensome hiring process.

Moreover, her late arrival—through no fault of her own—because a bus line was running behind can only be tolerated for so long before it rises to a level that requires reaction by Human Resources. On a more practical level, that same unavoidable tardiness disrupts the entire schedule for the whole day, not only for her but for the others she is scheduled to work with. And her inability to stay late in order to finish uncompleted assignments or cover for her fellow coworkers is likewise disruptive to the work schedule and workings of our facilities.

But Linda's situation is even worse.

If picturing your life without a private car seems to strain the limits of your imagination, try to picture completing your daily life activities without access to a financial institution or any of the many services that they offer. No debit card or credit card. No means of easily depositing pay checks. No ability to pay monthly bills directly from a personal account.

> **If picturing your life without a private car seems to strain the limits of your imagination, try to picture completing your daily life activities without access to a financial institution or any of the many services that they offer.**

The inescapable fact, is that, as of 2015, 7 percent of American adults do not have access to the ordinary services of a financial institution.[17] Many of my employees are among this number and during the course of our "listening sessions," I have heard time and again

---

17   "2015 FDIC National Survey of Unbanked and Underbanked Households," Federal Deposit Insurance Corporation, https://www.fdic.gov/householdsurvey.

about the unexpected consequences of being in such a situation.

When I point out this fact, all too many people ask me, "How could anyone not have a bank?"

I always take a deep breath and then respond by explaining to them that many of my employees—and many more of the citizens in the city that I call home—have a past history with financial institutions that prevents them from securing the services of a bank. Others regard the associated fees as an unnecessary or unaffordable expense. Many others simply don't understand the essential importance.

Yet without a bank account, they are prohibited from most legitimate rental situations, situations that would greatly improve their lives and allow for safer neighborhoods for their families.

The absence of a bank relegates them to using cash-paying servicers that take usurious advantages of those individuals, siphoning off as much as the law will allow from each hard-earned paycheck. Together, those situations create a sort of disability in our society that makes any sort of upward mobility a near impossibility.

Linda, for example, made some ill-advised financial indiscretions or mistakes in her early adulthood, leaving her unable to open an account at most standard financial institutions. As a result, even if Linda were able to somehow save or otherwise secure the down payment needed to purchase the car she needs so badly, she lacks the relationship with a lender necessary to make the purchase.

Without the opportunity to demonstrate that she has made amends with the mistakes of her past and is deserving of a financial second chance by remaining current and faithfully paying off a car loan, the difficulties she encounters in obtaining financial services continue.

Again, a vicious and seemingly inescapable cycle of financial instability and personal tribulations.

Again, the associated inconveniences and expenses connected to this disadvantageous situation are not reserved to Linda alone. As her employer, Loretto encounters several significant inconveniences in our interactions with employees who are similarly situated. For example, making the transition to a paperless pay system would offer a number of significant benefits to Loretto, but we are unable to take full advantage of these opportunities because of the number of employees who are not positioned to participate in such a program.

Enrolling in a paperless pay system would also be a great benefit at tax times when the requisite forms could be transmitted electronically rather than printed and sent via the mail. All of this costs Loretto money, just as it does Linda.

There you have it: past mistakes make it impossible for Linda to establish a relationship with a financial institution and, thus, she cannot get the loan she needs to purchase the car that would allow her to earn more money and improve her situation on all fronts.

At the same time, Loretto remains encumbered with an employee who—through no fault of her own—cannot be reasonably counted on to show up for her shift, cannot work extra hours when necessary, and is unable to advance within our internal schedule of promotion and professional advancement. We are, likewise, stymied from moving forward with making improvements to our own internal systems accordingly.

It's a lose-lose situation.

And yet, time and again, we have witnessed that by operating under the principles of pragmatic altruism, there is almost always a solution to the

> By operating under the principles of pragmatic altruism, there is almost always a solution to the problem that will benefit everyone involved.

problem that will benefit everyone involved.

Enter, Vicki O'Neill, president of the ACMG Federal Credit Union.

As a non-profit institution, ACMG has adopted a mission of providing affordable financial services to low-income individuals with whom more traditional financial institutions refuse to do business.

Recently, those ACMG financial services include auto loans for select employees of Loretto. Together, Loretto and ACMG have debuted an exciting pilot program that would enable certain employees to become qualified for an auto loan and purchase a vehicle that has the potential to transform their lives.

Back to Linda. Where she previously was trapped in a cycle from which there was no reasonable point of exit, she can now take the steps necessary to qualify for an auto loan that allows her to purchase the reliable vehicle she needs to improve her employment situation and, in so doing, her life. Of course, Linda's road to loan qualification will not be an easy one. (Nor should it be.)

As part of the program, Linda will be required to undergo an extensive financial audit of her life, including an exploration of the details of that less-than-immaculate financial past. She will have to devise a budget that will demonstrate just how she plans to meet her current bills and take on the extra burden of the auto loan and related expenditures, such as insurance, licensing, and gas and maintenance.

On top of all of this, Linda will undergo a rigorous financial counseling regime that will entail more than ten combined hours of one-on-one work with a financial expert who will offer her comprehensive lessons on personal financial planning and other related life skills that will not only allow her to secure the needed loan for that life-changing vehicle, but will also provide her the education and guidance that she needs so that she can continue to make sound financial decisions moving forward as her financial picture continues to brighten.

Admittedly, the ACMG/Loretto partnership auto loan program is still in the pilot stages and we have only serviced a limited number of Loretto employees. Nevertheless, the initial results only confirm what we have learned elsewhere regarding the powerful impact of pragmatic altruism. These test subjects have proven that with the right supporting structure around them, they are prepared to handle the responsibilities associated with limited controlled indebtedness of this variety.

Again, the ripples of benefits have spread beyond Linda and her fellow program participants, returning to both Loretto and ACMG.

Loretto has gained from participating in the program, first and foremost, in the way that it has improved relationships with employees. Our desire to participate in measures such as these which ostensibly have nothing to do with the actual day-to-day functioning has had a remarkable (but not unexpected) effect on how our employees relate to us.

Many of our people have never had anyone show any particular interest in their position or state, and so our commitment to take positive steps to improve their stations has provided us with a significant degree of credit in their estimation of their employers and their level of personal commitment to us. You'd be surprised what motivation can be generated from a willingness to help people secure a car loan.

And, of course, we have now expanded that percentage of our workforce that is positioned to arrive

> You'd be surprised what motivation can be generated from a willingness to help people secure a car loan.

at work reliably on time and to work overtime and extra shifts.

All of this is an incredible advantage to us as we continue to strive to provide the best possible care to all of our patients and program participants.

ACMG, for their part, has gained new customers and closed on new auto loans. The best part of that news is that as a nonprofit institution, all of the interest income that is generated from those ACMG/Loretto auto loans is reinvested into ACMG and redirected into their ongoing efforts to bring financial services to the economically disenfranchised.

Of course, the greatest beneficiaries of all are those employees such as Linda who have managed to successfully pass the rigorous pre-screening and educational program necessary to qualify for such a loan. She now has the guarantee of safely arriving at work at the time of her choosing, the option of working overtime and extra shifts to help her offset the cost of her new vehicle, and, most exciting of all, the chance to put her new-found freedom to use in pursuing occupational opportunities that have the potential to allow her to create an entirely new life for herself and her family.

There is one last advantage I see, although this is not reflected on any balance sheet item or captured in a program review analysis. That benefit is simply the emotional and psychological boost that is obvious in all of the program participants. Most (if not all) of these individuals not only had no prior access to an automobile, but they had no hope in their heart that they would ever have the possibility in their lives, never feel the exhilaration that all too many of us take for granted whenever we slide behind the wheel of our car, turn over the engine, and drive off wherever we want.

The sense of personal achievement that the program participants so obviously feel is infectious and irresistible. It makes them better employees, better caregivers, and I strongly suspect makes them better people, better family members, and better members of the community, too.

I think my friend and partner in the program, Vicki O'Neill, has a particularly deep understanding of the importance of this intangible impact. From the positions that we hold respectively, we are both painfully aware of our area's distinction as one of the most impoverished communities in the entire United States. We see the struggle that so many face not at arm's length, but from a much closer perspective.

And we are both committed, in our own ways and through the utilization of our corporate positions, to addressing that terrible situation and changing it for the better.

This program is the first of its kind in our area, but it is the seed from which a thousand other programs could spring, all of them helping and enabling all of the participants. And beyond them, the communities that serve them.

As Vicki points out, "There's no doubt that one person can make a difference and I certainly try to do part toward that end. But the obstacles we face as a community in Upstate New York are so significant that despite all the personal positivity and commitment, I don't think they can realistically be overcome by the acts of just a few, no matter how noble or well-intended. Instead, I think those individuals must focus on using their singular gestures as a means of inspiring others, of rallying more and more currently disengaged individuals until we can amass a populous movement of sufficient size and strength to bring about the significant changes that are so badly needed in this area.

"I'm not naïve enough to think that a few dozen car loans will be sufficient to accomplish all this, but I believe that they can be used as shining examples of what is possible when we work together. If they are not the force that we need, then perhaps they will serve as the spark to a hundred others like us who want to make a difference but feel that real change is beyond us all. I hope that we can inspire a movement."

I share Vicki's sentiments and hope.

Like her, I understand the limitations inherent in our wonderful experiment. I know that changing Linda's life and the lives of others like her won't solve all of the issues that must be addressed, but they are proof that change can be made.

They are additional confirmation that pragmatic altruism will return personal rewards to all those who participate with the common good in mind.

13

Times Are Tough All Over

The pattern of pragmatic altruism is not limited in any way. To the contrary, as we have discussed its application to the workplace and then beyond that to the greater community, so too can it be put into action on a larger scale and encompassing a larger area.

Cayuga County lies along the western of Onondaga County, where Loretto maintains its corporate offices and where the efforts we have discussed up to now have largely been focused. They are sister counties, similar in so many respects and yet uniquely different from one another.

While both Cayuga and Onondaga counties share the same sort of economic challenges that are endemic of the entire region, their demographic make-up is significantly different from one another. Onondaga, with the city of Syracuse at its heart, is overall an urban population with a significant percentage of minorities comprising its population. Cayuga, on the other hand, is almost entirely rural and its population is more than 90 percent white.[18]

18 "Cayuga County, New York," United States Census Bureau, https://www.census.gov/quickfacts/fact/table/cayugacountynewyork/PST045217

Of course, economic need does not respect boundaries of race or background, and rural Cayuga County has proven every bit as in need of help and support as its urban counterpart, Onondaga.

Enter the Allyn Foundation.

The Allyn Foundation is a significant philanthropic trust that has dedicated itself to funding programs that build strong families and vibrant neighborhoods throughout Central New York, especially programs that address community prosperity, early childhood development, and women's health issues. But in Cayuga County, the foundation's focus has included addressing the needs of at risk seniors, as well.

Cayuga's county seat is located in Auburn, a town of about twenty-five thousand that is dominated by the Auburn Correctional Facility, a maximum-security facility that is located in the city's center. That earns Auburn the catchy moniker "Prison City," which is not exactly a tag that most Chambers of Commerce would be eager to tackle.

There's the prison. A Wegman's supermarket. A hospital. But not much else. And for a time, that included sufficient seniors care. Because Loretto specializes in providing care for seniors, I am particularly sensitive to the role that these seniors facilities play in a community. I am, however, also equally attuned to the fact that far too many are dismissive of the crucial nature of that role. That is,

Because Loretto specializes in providing care for seniors, I am particularly sensitive to the role that these seniors facilities play in a community. I am, however, also equally attuned to the fact that far too many are dismissive of the crucial nature of that role.

until those services are no longer available.

Such a situation arose in Auburn, where a combination of factors resulted in the financial decline of the senior care facilities in the area and then eventually a merger and closure of one of them.

In any community, this scenario would create a series of negative ripples throughout the population, but in Cayuga County the average age is forty-two and almost 20 percent of the population is over age sixty.[19] By 2025, that figure is supposed to increase so that more than 50 percent of Cayuga will be over the age of sixty. For this county particularly, the results of losing a senior's facility was absolutely disastrous.

To understand the full ramifications of this situation, let's examine the repercussions on a single individual, Bob.

Bob was born and raised in Cayuga County, as most of the inhabitants of the county were. He married his high school sweetheart, raised a family, and worked at the prison for forty years until he retired at the age of sixty.

In another era, Bob might not have needed to worry about his "golden years," but those family and community protections are no longer in play.

Bob's wife passed away. Then Bob got sick. And he got sicker still, until he could no longer care for himself, and his daughter felt there was no other option but to place her father in the area senior's facility.

While this is a difficult decision for any family to make, it was doubly so for Bob's daughter because it was readily apparent that the facility was experiencing challenges in providing the care that seniors deserve. Those conditions continued to deteriorate until the facility was merged and the residents were moved to other facilities in the community.

---

19   Ibid.

The impact was devastating.

First, the residents, including Bob were displaced, which was a significant trauma to each of them.

Second, those individuals who had serious health issues then had to be taken to the local hospital, which put an enormous strain on the hospital's resources and their overall ability to serve the community. This, in turn, compromised the standard of care that was available to all those patients who utilized this facility.

And, finally, there was a significant impact on all of the residents' family members.

Bob's daughter could have been compelled to leave her job in order to stay home and provide the constant care that her father required. This, in turn, would put an enormous strain on the family that—like so many families in the area—was completely dependent upon two incomes. That's where the Allyn Foundation came in to save the day.

Meg O'Connell, head of the Allyn Foundation, has been instrumental in not only providing supporting funding for Loretto but in partnering with our organization in a number of projects throughout Upstate New York.

In this instance, when Loretto was asked to step in and participate in revitalizing the merged senior's facility and bringing it back to the standards that would allow for it to once again provide the senior services that were needed by so many in the community, The Allyn Foundation stood with Loretto as a partner.

Working together, we were able to restore the facility and today, it has returned to providing housing and badly needed services to the seniors of Cayuga County.

The effects have been every bit as positive as we had expected.

The significant financial pressures that had been placed on so many of the families of those who were facing loss of their senior services were effectively abated when their loved ones were allowed to remain at the facility. For example, Bob's daughter was able to retain her employment and continue to participate in the financial contribution that was so necessary to her family's financial well-being.

The pressures, both financial and in terms of staffing demand, that had been placed upon the local hospital were likewise lessened as patients were offered choices for more appropriate care situations.

And last, but certainly not least, the individuals themselves benefitted by being allowed to remain at a facility that served their needs even better than their loving families could.

This is yet another example of the widespread benefits that are realized when the focus is placed not necessarily upon the sort of immediate returns sought in profit-making endeavors, but which are available to funders and community alike when the intention is shifted to doing good. This does not, however, negatively impact the business considerations involved.

The Cayuga County facility has proven to be an important addition to the Loretto family of service providers.

The fact of the matter is that there doesn't need to be an either/or situation. To the contrary, the more we collectively look to the needs of those around us, the greater the returns that we are likely to realize.

As we move forward, Loretto and The Allyn Foundation are exploring a number of projects, including initiatives that are aimed at significantly improving child care opportunities and early childhood development resources for the youngest members of our community.

> The more we collectively look to the needs of those around us, the greater the returns that we are likely to realize.

Our intention is that by providing for these children, all of us—not just the children and their parents—reap long-term rewards for generations to come in the form of a generation that is better positioned to positively contribute to their community. Just a handful of programs, but the blueprint for a far greater community- and region-wide social reclamation. And this is exactly how we can achieve what so many have cynically dismissed as the impossible.

That is how we can forge a future that serves all of us.

Together.

14

A Brave New World

There are no limits or boundaries on the returns that can be realized from living our lives and conducting business within this spirit of pragmatic altruism.

I have seen first-hand how these principles in practice can produce incredible results in an individual's life, in a workplace, and throughout our communities.

Recently, however, I have seen how these same efforts can not only enrich our communities, but also provide a beacon that shines all around the world. Like the ripples of a pebble thrown into a pond, they spread out and repeat themselves over and again, without any boundaries, political or otherwise.

America is what is known in sociology and human geography circles as a "settler society." What that means is that with the exception of the Native American population—and Onondaga County has a sizable population from the Iroquois Nations— everyone in the United States can trace their heritage back to ancestors who made that courageous journey, often seeking to take advantage of the many opportunities to be found here, but more likely fleeing some form of oppression and/or persecution.

For many of us, that perilous journey was made many generations ago, but all too tragically, that same pattern of fleeing oppression and seeking liberty is still being played out today. Every year, more than a million people come to the United States as immigrants, giving our country the largest immigrant population of any nation in the world.

Personally, I see that figure as a source of tremendous national strength.

My hometown and Loretto's headquarter city, Syracuse, New York, has proudly (and defiantly) declared itself to be a sanctuary city at a time when the need for such protections have never been greater in modern memory. Because of this position, Syracuse—and Onondaga County, as a whole—has attracted a disproportionate number of both the refugees who are fleeing violence and oppression in their homelands and the immigrants who have come to the United States seeking to better their lives and the lives of their children.

It's a strong, vibrant, and diverse population and one that I am proud and pleased to have acquainted myself with intimately.

My introduction has come largely through my friend Chol-Awan Majok, who serves as the community engagement representative for New York State Senate Office of senator David J. Valesky, 53rd District. In this important role, he is fully aware of a situation that far too many people don't understand is playing out in plain sight. He is one of The Lost Boys of South Sudan who left his village at the age of eight when it was consumed by the unspeakable brutality of the Sudanese Civil War.

Chol now is a leader in the New American Forum, which is a public service organization working with these newest arrivals in

America to offer them a much-needed political and social voice and to assist them in integrating into the many strata of American society, including economically and educationally.

And in the first step in that process, Chol has made clear that it is essential to simply acknowledge this growing community and the harsh conditions that they frequently confront in their new home. "Poverty is what we live with every day," he says. "The majority of these people are looking to get out of this situation, but due to the lack of resources and access—especially access—giving these people opportunities and helping them with access to those opportunities is the key. That might just be the way forward. Partnership moving forward is the beginning."

Contrary to what might be portrayed on the politically slanted (one way or another) news or in social media, the main obstacle in achieving this objective isn't cold heartedness or xenophobic hatred. To the contrary, I believe that whatever the polls may claim to reflect, the American people—and by that, I mean individuals, neighbors, you and me—are extremely warm-hearted and welcoming by nature. The problem, as my friend has explained it to me, is simply that most Americans are unaware of the plights that these newest Americans face in the day-to-day of their search for the American Dream.

And while the lack of awareness extends throughout our community, the invisibility of the problem is most distressing among

> I believe that whatever the polls may claim to reflect, the American people—and by that, I mean individuals, neighbors, you and me—are extremely warm-hearted and welcoming by nature.

those corporate leaders who have within their direct control the means to address the situation in real and meaningful ways. So, the resolution of the problem is dependent upon opening a meaningful dialogue between the community power brokers and those who are most desperately in need of their intervention.

As Chol says, "A lot of CEOs want to live where they live, but where they live is not where the problem is. So, if a CEO like Kim Townsend decides to participate in this deliberation process, this discussion, this dialogue, that act of bravery encourages these other [CEOs] to become willing to change themselves and to understand the plight of the immigrant community by getting out of their comfort zones."

This dialogue and the tangible "real-world" results that would certainly be born from the process are needed sooner than later, however, as the situation among the ever-expanding immigrant population is not improving as quickly as it should and the always-widening void is creating a potentially disastrous situation for these specific individuals and for the community as a whole.

Chol has identified this simmering potential-disaster and the unexpected human consequences of this situation. "These people have been hurt. They have been hurt in many ways, including that they have been promised things, at some level, but things never changed. They continue to live in dangerous environments, they live in an environment that is dangerous to them and their children. They are disappointed with service delivery. So, people like myself who work with them every day are trying to tell them to look for the positive in this situation, we are in a very difficult position. If you can sympathize with them and be willing to be part of that journey with them, that is a start."

Under my leadership, that's exactly what Loretto has tried to do. Rather than ignore their plight and the potential solutions to their problems, Loretto has endeavored to become a companion with them on their journey.

Loretto has reached out to this community in a number of ways. The most immediate measure that has been undertaken is that we have made a concerted effort to hire from these pools of potential employees. And the results have been wonderful, far exceeding even our most optimistic expectations for the program.

There are many widely held misconceptions about the members of this diverse group, but one of the most pervasive—and tragically ill-informed—is that all of the immigrant community are undereducated and ill-suited for positions of employment in the United States. Too many are quick to dismiss and paint a community with a broad brush like "immigrants," when really they are an extremely diverse community with members who represent an astonishingly diverse range of backgrounds in all areas, including education and vocational training. While there are certainly individuals whose previous lives in their native countries precluded receiving a formal education, there are other members of that same community with extensive educations and career experience.

One of the shining lights

> Too many are quick to dismiss and paint a community with a broad brush like "immigrants," when really they are an extremely diverse community with members who represent an astonishingly diverse range of backgrounds in all areas, including education and vocational training.

of our hiring experience from this extraordinary talent pool is a woman who fled the generations of oppression in her native Cuba and brought with her the substantial medical education and experience that she received there before she made her departure. She has made a virtually seamless transition to our patient-care staff and it might be argued that her qualifications and capabilities far exceed what might be expected from any of her coworkers at that particular level of care.

There are admittedly others who have educational needs to prepare them for entering and/or fully realizing their potential within the work force, and Loretto is undertaking measures to play a meaningful role in these endeavors. Loretto is initiating programs in cooperation with the New American Forum to help fund educational initiatives for these individuals within the immigrant community.

Of course, one of the most significant obstacles that many of these new Americans face is the significant disadvantage of a lack of command of the English language. To address this fundamental need, Loretto and its partners are undertaking efforts to provide English language training to all of its employees and then, we hope, extend those programs beyond and out into the community. This is particularly important—and ambitious—considering that there are now more than eighteen separate languages spoken among our employees.

Again, I take my position as president/CEO of Loretto very seriously and I haven't sought out these opportunities merely because they are the right thing to do or because they serve some noble purpose. All of that is true, but my eye is always fixed on my organization's success, and my primary motivation in everything I do is to serve the corporation in the best possible way.

All of these programs in which I've enlisted Loretto accomplish both ends.

Loretto's experience in hiring from this particular labor pool has not only justified our investment, but has also provided demonstrable real-world advantages. The individuals whom we've hired have demonstrated an exemplary work ethic and professionalism.

There are a number of possible explanations for this result, but I think the most satisfying for me is that when a person has had a life ripped away from them—whether that was a result of a voluntary exodus in search of a better life or a far more tragic journey to escape violence and oppression—there is incredible gratitude for every act of assistance. Unlike some natural-born employees who may have come to take the simple liberty of a steady position of employment for granted, these newest arrivals to America seem to have a keen appreciation for how important that situation truly is and they express a gratitude each and every day that could well serve as a standard for us all.

I suppose that, ultimately, is the goal. Not only to integrate these people into American society, but to learn something from them in return and build a better and stronger community together.

That is the goal that I am committed to both as an individual and as a corporate leader, because the alternative—a failure to accomplish this—is an unthinkable outcome.

As my friend Chol put to me, and as he would have me challenge other executives in this community and similar communities across our great nation, "What am I doing as a leader of this community? What should I do to make sure that a child in this city is not going to bed hungry, is not living in a dangerous and threatening environment, to have a way to cope with this environment? What will I do to make sure that every child has an opportunity to participate in the American Dream?"

To me, the answer is a simple one: Everything that I can.

I would join my friend in extending that same challenge to others who are situated similarly to myself. The steps to be taken are really quite simple when broken down to their basic components:

Open your eyes and acknowledge everyone in your community.

Begin a dialogue.

Do what needs to be done.

I promise, the rewards will more than justify your efforts.

> Open your eyes and acknowledge everyone in your community.

15

The Future

n the course of preparing this project, someone asked me—in light of all of my work with Loretto to better life for our employees and the community that we share and call home—what I saw as the future for Loretto and my efforts in this regard.

The question somehow managed to catch me off guard, although I was aware even at the time that I should have had a ready answer to what I recognized was an obvious inquiry. Still, I needed a minute of reflection to fully consider the question before I could respond.

I can't fully explain the delay in offering my vision of the future. I think I am too focused on the present and making a difference today to give too much consideration to the far-off imaginings of what might (or might not) be waiting down the road.

Nevertheless, it was an interesting and important prospect for me to consider and I recognize that my efforts to address this multitude of present needs are tied inextricably to some shared plan for the future.

After this unexpectedly lengthy period of consideration, I concluded that while I might offer a more layered description of certain programs, what I really saw as the future for all of our efforts could be summed up into one very simple word: children.

Certainly, we at Loretto are doing everything that we can do to improve the lives of the women and men whom we employ, our program participants, and those with whom we share this community. But I think that when all is said and done, the true beneficiaries of all of the programs we have initiated and are rolling out in the days to come will be the children whose lives were directly and indirectly changed as a result.

I like to think that our efforts to provide a stable and supportive workplace for all of our employees will not simply benefit those who cash the paycheck but will also empower those children who were raised in homes in which a reliable income streams and a sense of hope and purpose created opportunities for them that perhaps their parents did not have.

I like to think that our efforts to provide a stable and supportive workplace for all of our employees will not simply benefit those who cash the paycheck but will also empower those children who were raised in homes in which a reliable income streams and a sense of hope and purpose created opportunities for them that perhaps their parents did not have.

I like to think that our efforts to create a diaper bank and accommodate child care needs of our employees provided an early childhood experience that was vastly improved from the situations that existed before our involvement. And I hope that these children reaped the rewards of those improvements across the whole of their childhood.

And "the children" is a wonderful summation of the particular programs that Loretto now has in the planning stages, with an eye on rolling out in the very near future.

. Perhaps the most exciting project that Loretto is considering is in conjunction with partners to build townhouses on our main corporate campus that would provide affordable, safe, child-friendly housing for those employees who are most in need of such a situation. Our intention here is not only to erect buildings, but to lay the foundations for true communities that would provide a mutually supportive environment in which all who would call it home could thrive, free from the challenges in the neighborhoods where so many of our employees currently reside.

While there is no doubt that the employees who would take up residence in these housing units would benefit from our efforts to provide them with dramatically improved residential situations, I like to think that those who would reap the greatest rewards will be the children who would have the opportunity to grow up in this special neighborhood.

In addition, as a part of these proposed residential communities, we are also exploring the creation of childcare facilities for our employees that would offer basic child care and crucial early-learning programs.

Certainly, this ready access to child care would be of a direct benefit to our employees who as (often single) parents struggle with the simple issue of child care while they work. These same parents likewise would benefit from the intervention of early-learning programs that will teach their children basic skills that they will certainly need for kindergarten and their first forays into the educational system.

Still, I like to think that the greatest beneficiaries would be the children themselves, who would have safe and reliable care when they are unavoidably away from their parents and a solid formative foundation upon which they would be able to grow to their fullest potential.

I like to think that these same children would grow up to be successful adults who find personal satisfaction in their life pursuits. And when they think back to their beginnings on the Loretto campus, I hope that they will pay forward their experiences by making significant contributions in the betterment of the lives of others.

In that way, I hope whatever foundations we pour and whatever we are able to build in brick and mortar will take root and give rise to something far greater than just buildings, far greater than even the sort of community I know that we can create for our employees. It is my fervent hope that with these facilities, we would be laying the groundwork for a self-perpetuating network of individuals dedicated to spreading pragmatic altruism in such a way that the rewards to those most in need spread and increase exponentially.

I am certain that there are some readers who will persist in dismissing my aspirations with suggestions that these plans have little or nothing to do with furthering Loretto's corporate goals and improving that all-important bottom line.

Intellectually, I certainly understand the source of this perspective, but I think it reflects a short-sightedness and an antiquated way of looking at a world that is changing in a myriad of ways and at a pace unseen previously.

Which, of course, is my way of saying that they are simply wrong.

The fact of the matter is that if these townhouses are built for employees, it will provide an environment will make them happier employees. Without the concerns that too many of our current employees must bring with them as they report for duty, the residents of our new facilities will attend to their daily duties more focused on the most important factor of all: providing the very best inpatient care.

And providing the highest quality patient care is Loretto's bottom line.

In that same way, I hope that the employee residential campus that we are now exploring will serve to inspire not only the residents that will come to call it home, but other corporate leaders who might look upon those buildings and see the same vision for the future that I do.

> Providing the highest quality patient care is Loretto's bottom line.

That would be the greatest of triumphs for me, because I'm aware of what it would mean in the future. The fact of the matter is that Loretto—despite its relative size and the important role in plays not only in our community, but in the entire region—is only a single player among many.

That, for me, is the most frustrating aspect of our endeavors. The funding obstacles and the everyday speed-bumps I can handle without any particular stress, but I am frustrated by the lack of progress in rethinking antiquated models of employee relations and community development.

I hope that our plans for the campus housing complexes and the other programs that I have outlined and discussed in this book will come to fruition to benefit the lives of those who have directly received but will serve as a challenge and motivation for others to follow our lead.

Together, all of the major corporations in our region working synergistically to improve conditions for our employees and all of the people with whom we share this wonderful community could accomplish amazing things, could make miracles mundane and ordinary.

The greatest rewards of all would be reaped by those same companies which participate in similar programs. A stronger community would certainly improve conditions for their employees, which I can testify would correspond to heightened performance in the workplace. And a strengthened local economy would undoubtedly produce the sort of black-ink, bottom-line rewards that these "pragmatists" would suggest are the only rewards worth pursuing.

That brings me back to those townhouses. They are currently little more than an aspiration, but I see them as something real. I see them as a potential source for great growth, for all of us.

I see them as the future.

16

One Final Story

Ever since I began my efforts at Loretto—and, happily, that first day as president/CEO now seems like it has been quite some time ago—I have received any number of reactions to Loretto's initiatives to better the lives of all of those with whom we are fortunate enough to share this workplace or community or world. Each of these responses, however, can generally be filed away into four very distinct groupings. The first two I have already discussed.

The first of these comes typically from some of *our employees* who are overwhelmed by one personal crisis in their life or another or more commonly by the cumulative effects of a tsunami of personal catastrophes. These people look at me, but understandably only catch sight of my title and what they perceive that must mean for me in my corner office where they think the world has no problems. They tell me, "You couldn't possibly understand. You're doing good things, you're trying, but that's just you trying to fix a problem that you could never understand."

The second response I receive is from those *executives* or people whose socio-economic status has protected them from walking those streets of despair and whose perspective prevents them from seeing clearly what is really happening in neighborhoods all around them. Rarely are they callous people, completely devoid of any meaningful human empathy. For the most part, they are people who think of themselves as kind and caring (and they're generally right about that) but they simply aren't aware of what happens in what is essentially another world.

Whether it's intended or not, I've often found that people in this second group hold the misconception that "*these* people" are different from us. They say things to me like, "I appreciate what you're trying to do, but there's only so much that can be done and you can't fix the world. It's like trying to empty the ocean into a bucket."

The response I get from a third group—and by far the most common—is simply "*Why?*"

I want to talk about this third group for a few minutes. No matter how many times I face this question, I can't help but be shocked when it's presented to me. I am always surprised that so many people seem genuinely mystified about our motivations when the answer to their question seem apparent to me.

Sometimes I answer, "Because every measure that we have undertaken for the betterment of others has carried with it a direct and significant real-world benefit to the success of Loretto's operations, resulting in demonstrable advantages realized on the bottom line."

Other times, I simply say, "It's the right thing to do."

Or my personal favorite, "Why wouldn't I?" But I have to admit that I have motivations even beyond these obvious one. And by answering that persistent question—*Why?*—I think I might finally be able to offer a definitive reply to those first two responses as well.

Why?

Why do I even bother to devote so much of my efforts as a corporate president/CEO to activities that seemingly do little else than help others? To answer that question, I present one final story.

The beginning of this tale is all too tragically common in a country in which even the most conservative figures estimate that more than 40 million children grow up in houses where they witness some form of domestic violence.[20] That shocking number skyrockets alarmingly when the parameters are adjusted to include children whose situations were marked with emotional distress and/or neglect.

The problem for too many of these kids is that there is no happy ending to their stories, and by that, I mean that there is no ending at all.

Instead of moving on to a better situation in their adult years, those who endure a childhood tainted by abuse often find that this disturbing experience becomes merely a training ground for the perpetuation of those same conditions later on in their adult lives. All too often, those victims are caught in those same terrible patterns of abuse and experience the same.

The subject of our story was a young woman who went from a less-than-ideal upbringing to a much-less-than-ideal relationship with a man who at first appeared to offer a way out of her unhappy adolescence, but then quickly became abusive.

A tragically all-too-common situation that repeats itself across this country every day.

The young woman was still young when she found herself married. And a mother.

Children are, of course, the greatest blessing that this life has to

---

20   "10 Startling Statistics about Children of Domestic Violence," Childhood Domestic Violence Association, February 21, 2014, https://cdv. org/2014/02/10-startling-domestic-violence-statistics-for-children.

bestow on any of us, but anyone who is trapped in an abusive relationship understands that these bundles of joys are also an anchor. Maybe you can run with one, but with two you're not going anywhere.

> Children are, of course, the greatest blessing that this life has to bestow on any of us.

And three. There's just nothing that can be done.

The subject of our story simply accepted the fact that she could not run from the abusiveness that marked almost every day.

But neither would she surrender to it.

So, eventually she went to find work. In no time, she realized that she could not provide for herself and her children in the sort of jobs that were offered to her without a college degree.

That deficit didn't stop her. Instead, she rolled up her sleeves and got busy. She took care of her children and worked whatever job she could while she went to college to get her degree.

And when that diploma was hers and she knew that she might be able to obtain a slightly higher-paying job, she decided that she would work even harder. She continued to balance the child care and the jobs, this time doing it all while she went to law school.

The law grad got a high-paying job that brought with it a degree of freedom from the oppressiveness that she had known for so many years, but even that wasn't enough.

She worked harder and harder, eventually earning a seat on the board of directors of a regional corporation. And when the president/CEO seat of that corporation fell vacant, she made the case for her candidacy and won that seat.

Yes, that is my story.

So, when people tell me that I don't understand what they're going through, I never express outrage. Of course, I know exactly what it's like to worry about child care, to be occupationally handicapped simply for being a mother. I understand. I understand so well that I cannot completely shake the memory of those experiences.

While I am proud to be an example that anyone can overcome the adversities in their life and make their future exactly what they want it to be, I am also a testament to the fact that you can never completely escape your past. To all of those who think that I don't understand your plight or situation because I now reside behind the office doors of the president/CEO, I will share with you the fact that every time someone comes to knock on those doors, I instinctively flinch the same way you do when there's an unexpected knock on your door at home.

We are siblings you and I, bound by a terrible legacy. I understand. And because I do, there is nothing that I want more than for all of you to understand that you can do the same. No matter what limitations you think you face, I promise you that they can all be overcome—not easily, but permanently. With the right frame of mind, you can take all of the steps necessary to better your own position.

And to those who may have thought that my educational pedigree or current socio-economic status placed me in some elevated position from which to look down on *those people*, let me make it clear right now that whatever assumptions you might have made about me because of the car I drive or the neighborhood I call home, you are completely misguided.

Whatever conclusion at which you might have arrived, let me

> With the right frame of mind, you can take all of the steps necessary to better your own position.

make perfectly clear that rather than looking down on those people, I am unspeakably proud to be one of *those people.*

In fact, my life mission is to become a leader of *those people.*

My goal is to organize people with life experiences like mine and lead them step-by-step toward a revolution of kindness and compassion that has no greater objective than to ensure that all of us—*all of us*—can fully enjoy a life free of abuse, deprivation, degradation, and ignorance.

And that, too, is my answer to the question, *Why?*

Why do I do what I do? Because I know what it is like to be in desperate need of help and not have anyone who will extend to you any assistance or support. Not even acknowledgment of your suffering.

I know what it is like when someone reaches out of that darkness to offer the help you need so badly. In the darkest of my days, there was no shortage of people who knew just exactly what I was suffering through. Family and friends, neighbors and colleagues. Lots of people were aware of what was happening to me and were content to simply turn a blind eye to my situation.

Then a friend came forward to offer me what she could: support, help with the kids, a kind word. It was solely because of her kindness and selflessness that I was able to survive those days.

So, *why* do I do what I do?

For all of the reasons I offered above, but most of all because I feel in my heart that I owe it to my friend.

I feel that I owe her to repay the kindness that she showed me by paying it forward not just to one single individual, but to entire communities and generations.

All of that leads me to the response that I get from a fourth group when the subject of Loretto's altruistic initiatives become the subject of conversation: Thank you. That's all. Just— "Thank you." It means the world to me.

The thanks are not just for what I am doing—that's certainly a very big component—but I understand being in that position, I remember, and I know that the thanks are simply for acknowledging them and their situations. It's a thank-you for nothing more than caring about them and, in so doing, validating them.

I remember when I was going through the worst of my experiences and only one friend was there to even acknowledge what I was going through. I cannot find the words to express that feeling, to describe what it was like to be suffering in that way and then to have people that I knew very well—family and close friends—look straight through me like there was no problem. The effect was devastating to me, because I couldn't help but identify so closely with my situation. In ignoring my plight, they reduced me to less than I was, dehumanized me.

So, when I have an employee stop me in the hall and smile while she quietly says, "Thank you," I understand just how much she's really saying.

And just how much it means. To both of us. And that's why I do what I do. That's why it's so important that I continue. And that others join in that same cause.

CONCLUSION

They tell me that the path my life has taken—from victim and *de facto* single mother to president/CEO of a major multi-million-dollar corporation—is an exceptional one.

I might humbly agree, but only so far as to the extraordinary nature of the adventure itself. My life, despite the dark chapters, has been a wonderful ride.

I believe in my heart—in fact, it's more than that—I *know* that absolutely every individual carries within them the potential to fully realize their dreams and make them a reality.

Some of us, however, need a hand in doing so.

I could argue that the reward of lending that hand is found in the satisfaction gained by playing some small part in helping someone realize their dreams, but I understand that there are some who might scoff at that type of remuneration.

So I will say that the rewards are even greater than that.

I have seen them reflected in all sorts of real-world ways. In improved employee retention figures that have decreased the associated costs of hiring and maintaining our workforce.

I have seen it pay dividends in transforming people from

dependency on social support payments to thriving members of the community who are not only independent but who become contributors to the local and national economies.

It is so easy.

The same results are available not only to nonprofit corporations like Loretto, but to for-profits, as well. In fact, I would argue that the potential rewards are even greater for for-profit corporations. The revenue streams that could be generated within those less-regulated and more-aggressive structures would certainly empower a host of programs and initiatives that would have the potential to effect real and dramatic change across communities, across the nation, across the world.

The single-minded focus on profit at all costs that has marked capitalism has persisted for centuries, but there are undeniable changes unfolding around us now that necessitate a reevaluation of that mindset. A new era is on the horizon and it necessitates a new way of considering what exactly constitutes good business.

Our economy is changing all around us, whether we want to admit what we can clearly see or whether we insist on turning a blind eye to the evolutionary processes and continue to deny that there is any need for action.

There is a real need to do something to address these mounting problems, to invoke real-world solutions before we reach a tipping

> Our economy is changing all around us, whether we want to admit what we can clearly see or whether we insist on turning a blind eye to the evolutionary processes and continue to deny that there is any need for action.

point of human despair and economic failure that prevents us from ever setting things right again—and from ever realizing the future that we must certainly be obligated to pass along to our children and future generations.

Pragmatic altruism and Lifecircle Leadership is the answer.

There is no need for any drastic legislative action or sweeping social reforms, just a recommitment by individuals and organizations to simply do the right thing and take care of one another, offering the assistance necessary not to enable those in need but to empower them. What is needed is simply a corporate doctrine that values and perpetuates human decency and little (and not so little) acts of kindness.

I would like to think that Loretto is in the forefront of this movement.

I know that Loretto is stronger and better positioned to take on the very real economic challenges of the twenty-first century because of these endeavors. Our workforce is the most dedicated and provides an unparalleled level of standard of care in our industry.

Revenues are up. Innovation is flourishing. And those results are available universally and across the board to whatever individual and/or corporation wishes to take advantage of those subtle but all so important philosophical shifts and behavioral adjustments.

I have seen firsthand that there is no need to compromise business interests in pursuing that path of generous abundance. To the contrary, I believe that I have demonstrated in my personal life and through the corporate performance that Loretto has consistently demonstrated in a challenging industry and adverse market, that there are real opportunities for all of those who are willing to commit themselves to the pragmatic altruism of Lifecircle Leadership.

ACKNOWLEDGEMENTS

would like to thank my dissertation chair, Dr. Michael Robinson, my dissertation committee member, Dr. Linda Doty, and my Dissertation Reader, Dr. Kimberly Vanderlinden, for their guidance and support through the dissertation process which formed the seeds for this book. They led me to examine a topic, satisfied by curiosity, around what constitutes exceptional leadership.

I would like to thank the team at Advantage|ForbesBooks—Wes Fang, Eyre Price, Lauren Delamater, and Nate Best—for their patience as they reviewed and re-reviewed every draft, work and thought.

I would like to thank Julie Sheedy, Loretto's vice president for marketing, who wrestled with every draft and question, not solely as part of her job, but because of our longstanding friendship which I probably taxed to the nth degree.

And I would like to thank Crystal DeStefano, who brought her expertise in what people want and need to hear. Without her insight, this book would be less on the mark.